W9-BNU-617

MAKERS OF MODERN SCIENCE

Niels Bohr

REVISED EDITION

MAKERS OF MODERN SCIENCE

Niels Bohr

Atomic Theorist

REVISED EDITION

RAY SPANGENBURG AND
DIANE KIT MOSER

CHELSEA HOUSE
PUBLISHERS
An imprint of Infobase Publishing

NIELS BOHR: Atomic Theorist, Revised Edition

Copyright © 2008, 1995 by Ray Spangenburg and Diane Kit Moser

All rights reserved. No part of this book may be reproduced or utilized in any form or by any means, electronic or mechanical, including photocopying, recording, or by any information storage or retrieval systems, without permission in writing from the publisher. For information contact:

Chelsea House
An imprint of Infobase Publishing
132 West 31st Street
New York NY 10001

Library of Congress Cataloging-in-Publication Data

Spangenburg, Ray, 1939–
Niels Bohr: atomic theorist / Ray Spangenburg and Diane Kit Moser—Rev. ed.
p. cm.—(Makers of modern science)
Includes bibliographical references and index.
ISBN 13: 978-0-8160-6178-5 (acid-free paper)
ISBN 10: 0-8160-6178-5 (acid-free paper)
1. Bohr, Niels Henrik David, 1885–1962. 2. Physicists—Denmark—Biography. 3. Physics—History. I. Moser, Diane, 1944– . II. Title. III. Series.
QC16.B63S63 2008
530.092—dc22 2008001196
[B]

Chelsea House books are available at special discounts when purchased in bulk quantities for businesses, associations, institutions, or sales promotions. Please call our Special Sales Department in New York at (212) 967-8800 or (800) 322-8755.

You can find Chelsea House on the World Wide Web at
http://www.chelseahouse.com

Text design by Kerry Casey
Cover design by Salvatore Luongo
Illustrations by Melissa Ericksen
Photo research by Suzanne M. Tibor

Printed in the United States of America

MP KT 10 9 8 7 6 5 4 3 2 1

This book is printed on acid-free paper and contains 30 percent postconsumer recycled content.

In memory of Margaret L. Notson Moser,
who always encouraged a love of ideas,
knowledge, and understanding

CONTENTS

Preface x
Acknowledgments xiii
Introduction xiv

1 **The Making of a Physicist (1885–1911)** **1**
Soccer and Science 5
Conversations Overheard 6
Duality: A Lifelong Theme 10
Plunging into Physics 12
Brilliant Beginnings and Loss 15

2 **Mysteries of the Atom (1911–1912)** **20**
Interlude in Cambridge 22
Criticizing the Great J. J. 23
Rutherford and the Story So Far 24
Doing Physics in Manchester 27
Teamwork: Rutherford and Bohr 30
Exploring Atomic Structure 32

3 **Birth of Bohr's Atom (1913–1924)** **37**
The Black Body Dilemma 39
Using Quantum Physics 42
The Story of Spectra 43
What Are Spectra? 45
Fate of a Paper: ". . . Atoms and Molecules" 48
A Look at Bohr's Model 49
Back to Manchester 52
Ripple Effect and Two Offers 54
Enter Einstein 55

4 **Bohr and Einstein: Battle between Friends (1925–1929)** **59**
Pauli's Exclusion Principle 60
An Unlikely Friendship: Wolfgang Pauli and Carl Jung 60
Wave-Particle Duality 62
Heisenberg: Uncertainty and Quantum Theory 64
The Clock in a Box 66

5 **The "Spirit of Copenhagen" (1930–1938)** **71**
Exploring Atomic Structure 72
Bohr and the Atomic Nucleus 73
The Physicists' Parody of Faust 75
Intellectual Heights at Bohr's Institute 77
Bohr v. Einstein: The Great Debate 77
Tragedy and a World at War 79

6 **Open Door to the Nuclear Age (1938–1945)** **83**
Lise Meitner's Insight 84
Heisenberg: A Question of Ethics? 86
Escape 88
Copenhagen, *the Play* 89
Physicists Called to Battle 90

7 **The Final Years (1945–1962)** **94**
Public Life: Search for a Better World 94
Letter to the United Nations 97
Physicists, Particle Physics, Openness, and Peace 99
Shrinking Circle of Friends 103
Niels Bohr and the Pursuit of Truth 105

8 **Rethinking Bohr's Physics** **107**
What Are Strings? 109
The Universe Both Big and Small 109
The Impossible Dream? 111

Conclusion: The Legacy of Niels Bohr **113**

Chronology 117
Glossary 121
Further Resources 125
Index 135

PREFACE

Science is, above all, a great human adventure. It is the process of exploring what Albert Einstein called the "magnificent structure" of nature using observation, experience, and logic. Science comprises the best methods known to humankind for finding reliable answers about the unknown. With these tools, scientists probe the great mysteries of the universe—from black holes and star nurseries to deep-sea hydrothermal vents (and extremophile organisms that survive high temperatures to live in them); from faraway galaxies to subatomic particles such as quarks and antiquarks; from signs of life on other worlds to microorganisms such as bacteria and viruses here on Earth; from how a vaccine works to protect a child from disease to the DNA, genes, and enzymes that control traits and processes from the color of a boy's hair to how he metabolizes sugar.

Some people think that science is rigid and static, a dusty, musty set of facts and statistics to memorize for a test and then forget. Some think of science as antihuman—devoid of poetry, art, and a sense of mystery. However, science is based on a sense of wonder and is all about exploring the mysteries of life and our planet and the vastness of the universe. Science offers methods for testing and reasoning that help keep us honest with ourselves. As physicist Richard Feynman once said, science is above all a way to keep from fooling yourself—or letting nature (or others) fool you. Nothing could be more growth-oriented or more human. Science evolves continually. New bits of knowledge and fresh discoveries endlessly shed light and open perspectives. As a result, science is constantly undergoing revolutions—ever refocusing what scientists have explored before into fresh, new understanding. Scientists like to say science is self-correcting. That is, science is fallible, and scientists can be wrong. It is easy to fool yourself, and it is easy to be fooled by others, but because new facts are constantly flowing in, scientists are continually refining their work to account for as many facts as possible. So science can make mistakes, but it also can correct itself.

Sometimes, as medical scientist Jonas Salk liked to point out, good science thrives when scientists ask the right question about what they observe. "What people think of as the moment of discovery is really the discovery of the question," he once remarked.

There is no one, step-by-step "scientific method" that all scientists use. However, science requires the use of methods that are systematic, logical, and *empirical* (based on objective observation and experience). The goal of science is to explore and understand how nature works—what causes the patterns, the shapes, the colors, the textures, the consistency, the mass, and all the other characteristics of the natural universe that we see.

What is it like to be a scientist? Many people think of stereotypes of the scientist trapped in cold logic or the cartoonlike "mad" scientists. In general, these portrayals are more imagination than truth. Scientists use their brains. They are exceptionally good at logic and critical thinking. This is where the generalizations stop. Although science follows strict rules, it is often guided by the many styles and personalities of the scientists themselves, who have distinct individuality, personality, and style. What better way to explore what science is all about than through the experiences of great scientists?

Each volume of the Makers of Modern Science series presents the life and work of a prominent scientist whose outstanding contributions have garnered the respect and recognition of the world. These men and women were all great scientists, but they differed in many ways. Their approaches to the use of science were different: Niels Bohr was an atomic theorist whose strengths lay in patterns, ideas, and conceptualization, while Wernher von Braun was a hands-on scientist/engineer who led the team that built the giant rocket used by Apollo astronauts to reach the Moon. Some's genius was sparked by solitary contemplation—geneticist Barbara McClintock worked alone in fields of maize and sometimes spoke to no one all day long. Others worked as members of large, coordinated teams. Oceanographer Robert Ballard organized oceangoing ship crews on submersible expeditions to the ocean floor; biologist Jonas Salk established the

Salk Institute to help scientists in different fields collaborate more freely and study the human body through the interrelationships of their differing knowledge and approaches. Their personal styles also differed: biologist Rita Levi-Montalcini enjoyed wearing chic dresses and makeup; McClintock was sunburned and wore baggy denim jeans and an oversized shirt; nuclear physicist Richard Feynman was a practical joker and an energetic bongo drummer.

The scientists chosen represent a spectrum of disciplines and a diversity of approaches to science as well as lifestyles. Each biography explores the scientist's younger years along with education and growth as a scientist; the experiences, research, and contributions of the maturing scientist; and the course of the path to recognition. Each volume also explores the nature of science and its unique usefulness for studying the universe and contains sidebars covering related facts or profiles of interest, introductory coverage of the scientist's field, line illustrations and photographs, a time line, a glossary of related scientific terms, and a list of further resources including books, Web sites, periodicals, and associations.

The volumes in the Makers of Modern Science series offer a factual look at the lives and exciting contributions of the profiled scientists in the hope that readers will see science as a uniquely human quest to understand the universe and that some readers may be inspired to follow in the footsteps of these great scientists.

ACKNOWLEDGMENTS

We would like to thank the many people who helped form this book, including Felicity Pors of the Niels Bohr Institute, our tireless editor Frank K. Darmstadt, excellent photo researcher Suzanne M. Tibor, and our ever-positive agent, Linda Allen. We would also like to thank physicist Shawn Carlson for reviewing the manuscript of the first edition and making many helpful comments.

INTRODUCTION

This book tells the story of world-renowned physicist Niels Henrik David Bohr, the founder of modern atomic theory. It was exciting, cutting-edge work—cerebral and challenging. He was very good at what he did. His model of the atom was creative, imaginative, and mathematically insightful—and it brought him the Nobel Prize in physics in 1922.

However, his influence grew even greater as the first half of the 20th century progressed. He persuaded Danish authorities to establish an institute for theoretical physics, which was inaugurated in 1921, and so began Niels Bohr's powerful secondary career as mentor to physicists a half-generation younger, who profited from his wisdom and built upon his strengths. They came from Germany, England, France, Belgium, Austria, and elsewhere to experience the atmosphere fostered there—the mix of students with complementary strengths, the endless all-night discussions, and the love of knowledge Bohr encouraged.

His stature and charisma brought bright and competitive students to Denmark, to the new institute he had instigated in Copenhagen. They were attracted by his insights into the rapidly evolving model of the atom, a building block thought by the ancient Greeks to be indivisible. Bohr and his students and colleagues began pushing the limits of their experiments and they soon blithely applied splitting off small particles of the "unsplittable" atom to learn about its deeply held secrets.

Like most scientists, Bohr had produced much of his most seminal work as a young physicist and, as also is often the case, Bohr's model of the atom was not an easy sell. At the University of Göttingen, a major university in Germany, the word had been bandied about that Bohr's work was just a way of excusing ignorance—a pretty negative report. However, when he had the chance to present the model himself, even speaking in halting German, the reaction was more favorable. After one of these early presentations about his model of the atom, fellow physicist Max Born remarked to a colleague that "this Danish physicist looks so like an original genius that I cannot deny there must be something to it." In Munich, Bohr received a warmer reception, thanks to Arnold Sommerfeld—whose enthusiasm for innovation led him to embrace Bohr's creativity. Even though he was a little skeptical, he told his students Bohr's mathematics held up to scrutiny and that, in itself, Sommerfeld said, was "unquestionably a great achievement."

Niels and his brother Harald, a mathematician, were athletic as well as cerebral, and the summer that Bohr took his model on the road in Germany, he and Harald went hiking in the Tyrolean Alps. The year was 1914, the year that war broke out suddenly with a German declaration of war against Russia. The two young men doubled quickly back through Germany and took a ferry home to Denmark, just in time. Several years passed when Bohr was forced by the circumstances of war to abandon communication with the very allies he had just made among the group of young German physicists. It would be years before he would see some of them again. This constriction of the open exchange of information among scientists happened twice to Bohr. The second time would be much worse, but between the two World Wars, much cerebral activity took place among physicists, particularly in Denmark, Germany, and England.

From the moment they met in the 1920s, Albert Einstein and Niels Bohr began a lifelong friendship of conversation and debate about their differing opinions on quantum theory and quantum mechanics. They continually poked and prodded at the questions not yet answered and new questions kept coming up. They drew diagrams for each other and sought to convince each other.

This brilliant period of unbridled discussion did not last long though. Adolf Hitler came to power in Germany in 1933 and with him came autocratic rule. By the late 1930s, life in Germany was no longer safe for many people because of blatant and horrifying persecution of Jews. Millions of men, women, and children were shipped to concentration camps and executed. Many scientists fled Germany, including Albert Einstein. Bohr brought many people out of Germany through Denmark and found them places to stay, in the institute or in his home. It was the beginning of another era of his career, the use of his influence to promote peace, displaying his deeply held humanitarianism and personal courage. After World War II, Bohr used his influence to campaign for international treaties against the use of nuclear weapons and wrote an "Open Letter to the United Nations," which called for caution in production of atomic weapons and encouraged development of peaceful uses of nuclear technology. These campaigns were the natural extension of his lifelong concern for the responsible use of the advancement of science and the place of science in society.

This revised edition of *Niels Bohr: Atomic Theorist* offers new sidebars on topics of interest, such as the tools of physics and biographical profiles. There is also new material concerning the strange visit in 1941 by Werner Heisenberg of Germany to see Niels Bohr in Copenhagen during the German occupation of Denmark. To what purpose? No one really seems to know, but some experts think that Heisenberg was attempting to find out from Bohr what progress, if any, the Allied nations had made in developing an atomic bomb. A sidebar explores *Copenhagen,* the highly acclaimed 1998 play that probes some of the ethical concerns—still pertinent today—that surrounded Heisenberg's conduct and the relationship between science and society in the event of war. Finally, a new final chapter takes a look at string theory, the prevailing hypothesis (as this intellectual endeavor might more accurately be called) that fascinated physicists in Niels Bohr's field have turned to in an attempt at solving the paradoxes that raised so many questions in Bohr's time.

1

The Making of a Physicist

(1885–1911)

The cold late-winter wind of 1948 swept through the sparse woods behind the Institute for Advanced Study a few miles outside of Princeton, New Jersey. On the institute grounds that late afternoon only a few solitary walkers could be seen scurrying from building to building. A battered old car backfired a short distance away as it pulled up in front of Fuld Hall and discharged a passenger, a tall young mathematics professor with a hurried air. With his coat collar turned up against the wind, he rushed inside to the red-brick warmth of Fuld Hall, carrying an overflowing armload of books and papers from the nearby Princeton University library.

The Institute for Advanced Study, founded in 1930, had been established, as the founders' letter explained, to foster "the pursuit of advanced learning and exploration in fields of pure science and high scholarship to the utmost degree that the facilities of the institution and the ability of the faculty and students will permit," with the emphasis, from the beginning, on the word "advanced."

Although the founders had envisioned a kind of supergraduate school, where the brightest faculty minds would be free to pursue their own studies while teaching only a hand-picked group of graduate students, in reality the institute never enrolled a single graduate student. Its "students," instead, were its own brilliant and gifted members, an international community, all holders of the highest degrees and honors, the best scientific minds in the world. Freed from nonacademic distractions and responsibilities, the institute's members could concentrate solely on their own work, and they eagerly listened to and taught not undergraduate or graduate students, but one another, exchanging ideas with the best of their peers.

Not surprisingly, the institute drew many of the world's finest scientific and scholarly minds, both for long-term stays and shorter visits. In 1947 the "father of the Atomic Bomb," J. Robert Oppenheimer, had become the institute's third director. Under his leadership, as under the two previous directors, the big comfortable offices in Fuld Hall continued to be a thriving beehive of esoteric and often bewildering intellectual activity.

On that particular late-winter afternoon in 1948, perhaps its most prestigious resident member was Albert Einstein.

The young mathematics professor just in from the cold hurried through the office corridors with his armload of books and his hair still mussed from the wind, glancing in the open door of Einstein's cluttered office. He had promised to drop off some papers, but no one was in. He would drop them off later.

On another floor, in another part of the building, Einstein was also on the minds of two other men. The younger of the two, Abraham Pais, a young scientist wearing horn-rimmed glasses, sat at his desk, watching. The other, an older man with a large stocky frame and the drooping face of a big, friendly bulldog, paced the room. The older man muttered softly, his thick Danish accent making his words almost unintelligible. He was visibly upset. He had jammed the pipe he usually smoked into his pocket, and he seemed to be struggling even more than usual for the right words. Finding them hardly seemed a relief.

"I am . . . I am . . . sick of myself," he muttered finally, giving the younger man a frustrated look before stalking back to stare out the window at the late-afternoon sky.

The younger man watched sympathetically. It wasn't the first time that he had witnessed Niels Bohr's frustration after one of his long and difficult discussions with Einstein. It might not have been as hard if the two men hadn't cared so much for each other.

"I am as much in love with him as you are," Einstein had once written about Bohr to a friend. In another letter, to Bohr after their first meeting, he wrote, "Not often in life has a human being caused me such joy by his mere presence as you did."

But, despite their affection, their heated and complex intellectual debate had gone on now for over two decades and neither had managed to change the mind of the other. Each was completely certain that he was right. And with that certainty came constant frustration over their mutual inability to convince the other.

A bubbling cauldron of intellectual energy, Niels Bohr didn't take frustration easily. Pais remembered Bohr's arrival at the institute only a few weeks before. Bohr had taken a ship from his home in Denmark. Finding himself aboard without anyone to discuss his ideas with, he had practically exploded from the frustration. Niels Bohr was a man who needed to talk. The first people he saw in the institute's corridors had been Pais and Wolfgang Pauli, and he had quickly hustled them into an office, and after silencing the talkative Pauli, proceeded to unravel all the thoughts collected during his ocean voyage. Pais later remembered wishing that there had been a stenographer handy. Bohr's conversation was a veritable history book on the evolution of ideas about the atom and its structure, ideas that had forever changed most physicists' views about reality.

Actually, "conversation" was a misleading word. It had been more of a mumbled, occasionally hesitant, but always brilliant monologue, with even the usually argumentative Pauli sitting quietly and listening, spellbound.

Now, though, Bohr stood silently at the window. Perhaps he hoped to catch a glimpse of Einstein on the grounds. Einstein, who it seemed had haunted his mind ever since that first meeting in Berlin in 1919. Einstein, who would never agree with the ideas that Bohr felt so terribly strongly about, who would never see the world in the way that Bohr saw it. Einstein, who would continue to go his lonely and individual way.

The big Dane shrugged his bulky and still-athletic shoulders. He would never win Einstein over. Never. Never! And yet . . . And yet . . .

The young mathematics professor dumped his armload of books onto his desk. He was running late and was in a hurry to wrap up his errands and get home for dinner. The wind was blowing harder and was rattling the window of his office. A storm was coming and he didn't like his wife to drive in bad weather. If he could get back downstairs, he could catch her in time before she parked the car and came looking for him in the building.

He caught a movement in the corner of his eye. Glancing up, he saw the familiar shaggy-haired figure walk past the open door. He started to call out, checking his desk to make certain that he still had the papers Einstein had asked him to pick up. When he looked up again, he could no longer see the baggy gray sweater. He debated with himself briefly. Did you chase Albert Einstein? He moved to the door and looked out into the corridor, but he had acted too slowly. The shaggy figure had vanished around a corner.

Outside the institute, the skies had darkened and the wind had picked up. Lights were going on in many of the offices. In a window on one of the upper floors, Niels Bohr stood silently staring out at the wind-swept grounds.

A dozen windows away, another light flicked on. Packing the pipe that his doctors had forbidden him to smoke with tobacco he had "borrowed" from one of the other offices, Albert Einstein moved to the window and stared out.

On the grounds below a horn honked. The car door opened for the hurried young professor—and Einstein and Bohr returned to their thoughts. They would still be puzzling for hours to come. Neither would sleep well that night. And tomorrow they would try again.

What was this argument all about, an argument that engaged two of the most brilliant scientists of the twentieth century in a heated debate that Robert Oppenheimer once called "the richest and deepest dialogue since Plato's *Parmenides*"? A debate about nothing less than the nature of reality. And who was Niels Bohr, this tenacious but gentle bulldog of a man who for over two decades engaged in this great intellectual debate with Albert Einstein?

Soccer and Science

It was an important game between the world-famous Danish soccer team and the top-notch team from Germany. The Danes were attacking strongly on the German end of the field, when the direction of play turned suddenly toward the Danish team's goal, the ball careening down the field, amid fast-moving knees, legs, and elbows. Both teams followed in hot pursuit, when suddenly a panicked shout came from one of the stars on the Danish team. Their own goalie, he had noticed, was paying no attention at all!

Roused by the yell from his brother Harald, the goalie suddenly snapped into action, blocked the ball, and stopped the German drive. Meanwhile, the mathematical problem that he had been figuring on the goalpost waited for another onslaught by the tireless and unstoppable Niels Henrik David Bohr.

The story is one that citizens of Copenhagen love to tell about the rangy, heavy-jowled young physicist with the kind eyes, soft voice, and razor-sharp mind—it's somehow symbolic of Niels Bohr's uncanny ability to be everywhere and do everything at once. And to bring out the best in everyone around him at the same time.

Far from the clichéd image of the absentminded, unworldly scientist (as the public tended to imagine his friendly antagonist Albert Einstein), Niels Bohr loved people. He also felt strongly about issues and delighted in intense discussion and argument. He was aggressively and good-naturedly engaged in the world. Admittedly, there were times when Bohr appeared absentminded—one famous physicist today is the proud owner of a piece of charred chalk that Bohr tried to light, mistaking it for his cigar while lecturing at a blackboard. But not because he lived in an ivory tower—rather, because he had focused so intensely and completely on communicating some difficult idea to a befuddled but absorbed listener.

Next to science and sports, Niels Bohr loved most to talk. In fact, he needed to talk. Many of his friends and colleagues joked that conversation with Niels Bohr was often one-sided, with Bohr doing most of the conversing. Talking was as important as breathing to Bohr. Many scientists do their best work alone at a blackboard or in a lab. Some develop their most profound ideas lost in their own thoughts while walking through gardens or woods, or even lying in bed in the middle of the night. Niels Bohr did his best thinking in the heat of discussion.

Conversations Overheard

Bohr had learned the technique as a child, sitting with his brother on the floor of the family living room in Copenhagen and listening to his father and his friends talk. It was not just ordinary everyday conversation that Niels and his brother Harald listened to. Their father, Christian, was a professor of physiology at the University of Copenhagen, an articulate and famous physician deeply interested in science, art, and philosophy; his friends were among the intellectual elite of Copenhagen.

Christian Bohr was politically and socially progressive. Considered somewhat radical in his time, he was a religious skeptic and an early advocate of women's rights. But he still held a deep reverence for the past and its great thinkers. One of his particular favorites was the German philosopher Goethe, whose writings he often read aloud to his children. He was also a sports enthusiast who kept up with all of the latest scores in English football (soccer) games and was instrumental in introducing soccer, then little known in Denmark, to a wider audience.

The lively Bohr household was kept running smoothly by Niels's mother, Ellen, a gentle woman whose quick intelligence and loving nature embraced not only the immediate family but the many visitors who came to the Bohr home. As a result, Niels and his siblings grew up in an intellectual and social center for many of Copenhagen's liveliest minds.

Niels's father was also the son of a teacher, Henrik George Christian Bohr—Niels's paternal grandfather—who had headed an elementary school on the island of Bornholm, in the Baltic Sea south of Sweden. Christian was born in Copenhagen in 1855 and published his first scientific paper at the age of twenty-two, taking his medical

Family life and intellectual conversation were important to the Bohr family. Here, at age four, Niels Bohr (right) sits for a portrait with (left to right) his sister, Jenny, his brother, Harald (on his mother's lap), and Ellen Adler Bohr. (Niels Bohr Archive, Copenhagen)

degree in 1878 and receiving his Ph.D. in physiology two years later. In 1881 he married one of his students, Ellen Adler, the daughter of a prosperous Jewish banker and politician. Their first child, Niels's elder sister, Jenny, was born on March 9, 1883. Their second child, Niels Henrik David Bohr, followed soon after, on October 7, 1885. The third, Niels's beloved younger brother, Harald, was born on April 22, 1887.

Christian and Ellen spent portions of the early years of their marriage in the large and stately town house owned by the Adler family at 14 Ved Stranden in the heart of Copenhagen. Here Jenny and Niels were born. It was a charming place, surrounded by tiny shops and bookstores and colorful, cluttered rows of red-tile-topped houses. Here young Niels first began to form his strong and loving attachment to Denmark.

Across the street from the Bohr home stood a statue of Bishop Absalon, the Danish soldier, statesman, and prelate who had originally founded the town of Copenhagen as a fortress in 1166. Christianborg Palace, the seat of the government, faced the family's impressive stone-fronted house, and only a short distance away the mooring known as Christianborg Slot was home to the colorful fishing boats that traveled the busy Frederiksholms Canal to the harbor. Despite its damp and often rainy weather, Copenhagen was a bustling and picturesque city. It captured Niels early and held him spellbound throughout his life.

The Bohr family was well-to-do. In 1886, shortly after Christian was appointed associate professor of physiology at the University of Copenhagen, the young family moved into a luxurious and spacious apartment adjoining the university, previously occupied by Christian's predecessor. It was here, at Bregade 62, that Harald was born, and where Niels and his brother and sister lived happily through the remainder of their childhood days.

Christian Bohr encouraged his children by providing opportunities for them to explore their interests. Their summers were spent running and playing at their grandparents' summer home, Naerumgaard, just north of Copenhagen. Niels and Harald often passed their after-school hours with woodworking projects in a shop set up for them by their father in their home. The Bohr children grew up in an environment that encouraged independent development, humane compassion, and culture. Above all, Christian and Ellen Adler Bohr passed on a great love of knowledge and its pursuit.

At a young age, Niels seemed to have a good conceptual sense of the physical world, with a remarkable early interest in reflecting it accurately. One day when he was about three years old, Niels was walking with his father, when the physiology professor began exclaiming about the way a nearby tree's trunk extended up into branches and the branches into twigs, hung with leaves. "Yes," said little Niels, "but if it weren't like that, there wouldn't be any tree!" And as a fifth-grade student, he painstakingly completed an assigned drawing of a house, only after counting the number of pickets in the fence and representing them exactly in his carefully drafted production. While many people considered Harald to be the brighter of the two boys, Christian Bohr recognized Niels's unique qualities of imagination, always maintaining that Niels was "the special one of the family."

Little, if any, jealousy existed between the two brothers. They could never say enough in praise of each other, and were inseparable in childhood and best of friends throughout adulthood.

In later life, Niels's best friend, Ole Chievitz, would assert, when asked what characteristics of Niels Bohr he would rate the highest: "His goodness . . . Let us not give examples. Bohr would not care for that. You must be satisfied with my word when I tell you that he is as good in big things as in small. I am not exaggerating just because it is his birthday when I say that I consider him the best human being in the world."

But as a child, and even as a young man, he certainly was not a saint. He got into fights and angrily knocked flat anyone who offended his keen sense of justice—often administering a black eye or two. As a boy, young Niels was perpetually in motion, described by those who knew him as a "tornado," full of energy and mischief.

Niels was not always first in his class, according to the memories of his classmates, but he was regularly third or fourth from the top. Although he was outstanding in mathematics and science, for him, writing assignments were another matter, and writing remained an agonizing task throughout his life. Most difficult of all was concluding a piece. For Bohr, there was always more to be said, and the convention of ending with a summary baffled him completely. To him, summaries seemed redundant, repeating unnecessarily, he thought, what had already been said. He finished one early childhood essay on the topic of metals with the sentence "In conclusion, I would like to mention uranium." In later life, someone once asked his brother Harald, by then a well-respected mathematician, how it happened that he had succeeded in building a career as a lecturer, whereas Niels never had. Harald replied, "Simply because at each place in my lecture I speak only about those things which I have explained before, but Niels usually talks about things he means to explain later."

All three Bohr children continued their education at the university. Jenny studied history at the University of Copenhagen and

English at Oxford. After passing a teachers' examination in 1916, she pursued a career teaching history and Danish. For Harald and Niels, too, a university education was the natural, expected follow-up to completion of their studies at Gammelholm School, the elementary and high school they both attended.

Duality: A Lifelong Theme

In 1903, Niels entered the University of Copenhagen, where he and his brother played on the soccer team. Harald was definitely the better soccer player—later playing halfback on the 1908 Danish Olympic team (winner of the silver medal). Niels, though an avid and excellent athlete, only served as reserve goalkeeper on the university team. But, for Denmark, the Bohr brothers were champion "footballers."

During these years, Niels developed a natural ear for poetry and memorized many stanzas in German and Danish. In addition, he enjoyed reading philosophy—including the Danish philosopher Søren Kierkegaard—and fiction, and he especially valued a little book by the Danish writer Poul Martin Møller, *Tale of a Danish Student.* Bohr was always fascinated with the attempts Møller's student had made to sort out the many dualities inherent in life. As Møller wrote,

> *Thus on many occasions man divides himself into two persons, one of whom tries to fool the other, while a third one, who in fact is the same as the other two, is filled with wonder at this confusion. In short, thinking becomes dramatic and quietly acts the most complicated plots with itself, and the spectator again and again becomes actor.*

The last line, in particular, often found its way into Bohr's conversations. And this fascination with duality—two things at once—would fill his thoughts, even his thoughts of physics, throughout his life.

At the university, Harald and Niels took a philosophy class from their father's friend Harald Høffding and, following their father's tradition, formed a discussion group with some of their classmates. They met over coffee or beer and often discussed the problems raised in Høffding's classes—their conversations frequently dominated by Niels, who held forth in his often-mumbling manner, his listeners constantly entreating him with pleas of "Louder, Niels."

Close friends from boyhood through adulthood, Niels Bohr (right) and his brother, Harald, are shown here as students. (Niels Bohr Archive, Copenhagen)

Plunging into Physics

By 1905, at the age of 19, Niels was ready to plunge into the world of physics. The Royal Danish Academy of Sciences and Letters had proposed an award for the best paper on the surface tension of liquids, and Niels decided to enter. Lord Rayleigh, who was a major figure in physics at the time, had proposed that it was possible to figure out the surface tension of a liquid if a few factors were known. If one could take measurements of the length of the waves that formed on a jet of the liquid—such as might be produced by the nozzle of a hose—and one knew the speed of the jet and its cross section, then it would be possible to determine the amount of tension present on the surface.

Niels's father, delighted with his son's ambition, gladly volunteered the facilities of his physiology laboratory for the project. For months Niels spent long night hours—when no one would disturb the quiet he needed—producing perfect streams of water. By heating and drawing his own glass tubing, he had devised a method for producing a jet of water that would always have the same speed and cross section. And he spent hours measuring and remeasuring.

Finally the deadline was nearing, and he had not begun to write. His father—seeing that Niels had become mesmerized by his experiments and probably would never finish without intervention—packed his son off to the Adler summer home to write, far away from interruptions and temptations to experiment further. The ploy worked. His triumphant paper, though inconclusive, raised important questions, extending Lord Rayleigh's basic theory about the surface tension of liquids. Niels Bohr was declared one of two winners in the competition, and four years later, in 1909, the British Royal Society published the paper, translated and in modified form, in its *Philosophical Transactions,* a heady triumph for such a young scientist, especially for work done while still a college undergraduate.

It was an auspicious start. Bohr had begun, by accident, with a subject that would lead unexpectedly, 35 years later, to an understanding of how an atomic nucleus might split, opening a door to the tremendous explosive power of an atomic bomb and the development of nuclear energy.

By this time Bohr had begun to immerse himself in the key issues of modern physics. The hottest new topic in the journals, he found, was radioactivity—the talk of all the scientific circles in France, Germany, and England. And so for his required student presentation on some aspect of his field, Bohr settled on radioactivity.

Much of the hubbub had begun when Niels was about 10. During the 1890s, scientists were fascinated with cathode rays. If nearly all the air from a glass tube sealed with metal plates at each end is removed and then the metal plates are connected to a battery, the emptiness in the glass tube glows. The glow stretches from the negative (cathode) plate to the positive (anode) plate, and that's why the rays so produced are called cathode rays. (With a few adjustments, this is the principle of today's television tubes.)

In 1895 in Bavaria, Wilhelm Conrad Röntgen was preparing for some experiments with cathode rays when he discovered a strange new ray being emitted through the heavy black paper he had placed over his cathode ray tube. The ray caused a piece of paper coated with barium platinocyanide (used in photography) to glow. He found that the new ray could travel through walls. When he placed his hand in the ray's path, it passed through the flesh of his hand but not the bones, which appeared as dark rods in the brightness. He called the ray "X-ray," "x" for unknown.

In England, at the Cavendish Laboratory at Cambridge University, the physicist J. J. Thomson began investigating these issues. By 1897 Thomson had proved that cathode rays were not light waves, as many scientists had assumed. These were negatively charged particles, he showed, that virtually boiled off the negative cathode and sped straight for the positive anode, propelled by electrical attraction. He showed that a narrow beam of cathode rays could be deflected in both an electric and a magnetic field. What, then, could the cathode ray be composed of?

Thomson came up with an idea that shook the very foundation of physics and chemistry. These rays, he asserted, must be made up of particles that he called "negative corpuscles" (later renamed "electrons" by the Dutch scientist Hendrik Lorentz). What's more, Thomson said, they must be part of matter itself, part of the atom.

To physicists and chemists alike, all over the world, these pieces of evidence began the call for a new vision of the atom, the indestructible building block of all matter. The atom was a very old idea, dating back to the fifth century B.C., when two Greek thinkers,

Leucippus and his student, Democritus, first described it. All matter, they said, was made of fundamental particles that could not be split into parts. They called these particles "atoms." (The Greek word *atomos* means "indestructible.") These tiny, indestructible particles were the very essence of matter, they said. And each element, such as gold, silver, hydrogen, and so on, represented a single substance composed entirely of only one type of atom. Over the centuries this atomic theory seemed to fit experimental results consistently, and by the early 19th century most scientists had concluded that it depicted an accurate view of reality. By 1895 about 76 of these elements were known, and a Russian scientist by the name of Dmitry Mendeleyev had observed common traits among some of them when he arranged them by atomic weight (the weight of a single atom of an element). He called the arrangement he came up with the "Periodic Table of Elements." With only a few alterations, his periodic table is still in use today.

But now J. J. Thomson measured his electrons and found that they were much lighter than hydrogen atoms, the very smallest atom of all. (His first measurement put the new particle at 1/770th the mass of hydrogen, but a later measurement of 1/1840th proved more accurate.) However, according to the prevailing atomic theory, nothing could be smaller than the hydrogen atom. He also found that it didn't matter whether the cathode tube contained a vacuum or was pumped with any kind of gas you could imagine. His electrons were always the same.

Meanwhile, Röntgen's discovery intrigued Henri Becquerel, a Parisian expert on fluorescence, which is the natural tendency of some substances to glow. Becquerel knew that sunlight can induce fluorescence in some substances, and he decided to try some experiments with various materials. He decided to begin with a uranium salt, but met with a series of cloudy days and so, to save the materials for a sunny day, he wrapped the uranium substance in paper and stuck the package in a drawer with the unexposed photographic plates. When he retrieved the materials, he was amazed to find that the uranium salt had exposed the photographic plates, even though the salt was completely hidden from any light. He had discovered, quite by accident, that some substances give off another ray, similar to X-rays, but not the same. The year was 1898. Marie Curie, a talented young physicist working in Paris at the time, gave the name "radioactivity" to this newfound emanation.

The implications of these discoveries, when closely examined, set late 19th-century science into a great stir. Where did these rays come from? What were they? Thomson had already assailed the idea that atoms were the smallest unit of matter. Now, with the discovery of radioactivity, the Greek atom was called even more into question. Where could these rays be coming from other than from the atoms themselves? If pure samples of an element could emit rays, the atoms must be disintegrating in some way; that is, the rays must be composed of *part* of the atom. But atoms, by the old Greek definition, had no parts. An atom, according to Leucippus and Democritus, was unsplittable. With the discoveries of Thomson, Röntgen, and Becquerel, the ancient Greek view of the atom as solid and unsplittable had come to an end.

This was the kind of dilemma physics was facing when Niels Bohr prepared his paper on radioactivity. He had picked out the very area of physics that was at that moment just ready to burst into hundreds of new avenues of investigation.

Brilliant Beginnings and Loss

Niels received his bachelor's degree from the university in 1907 and continued on as a graduate student to work on his master's degree. For his thesis work, he chose the subject of the electron theory of metals. By 1904, Thomson had set forth, based on his discovery of the electron, a revolutionary new vision of the atom—often referred to as the "plum pudding" or "raisin-in-pound-cake" model. An atom, he said, was primarily a positively charged sphere, embedded with negatively charged electrons, much as raisins are embedded in a plum pudding or pound cake. These electrons, researchers began to realize, determined how elements combined, and it began to become apparent that all chemistry was ultimately a matter of electrical attractions. Niels, working very near the cutting edge of his field, was exploring how the theory of electrons related to the characteristics of metals.

Meanwhile, Harald, back from the Olympics, moved steadily forward to work on his own master's thesis in mathematics, finishing before his brother, in 1909. Harald then set off for the university at Göttingen, where the most advanced work in his field was taking place. Niels, who was still laboring over his thesis in June 1909, was both a little jealous and very proud.

Upon his return to Denmark, Niels Bohr and Margrethe Nørlund married. This is a photograph taken at the time of their engagement in 1911. They were close companions for the rest of their lives. (Niels Bohr Archive, Copenhagen)

Once again, for Niels, writing the thesis would require getting away from the temptation to continue researching and experimenting. Upon his grandmother's death, her home at Naerumgaard had been given away by the Adler family to become a children's home, so it was no longer available as a retreat. Niels went instead to a vicarage located on the island of Fyn, one of the main islands of Denmark. It was the home of the father of Christian Bohr's assistant, Holgar Mollgaard, and it turned out to offer the isolation and opportunity for focus that Niels needed for his writing. There he pored over the books and articles of Thomson, as well as publications by Paul Drude and Lorentz. He succeeded in homing in on assumptions and uncovered a few discrepancies in Lorentz's work (as he wrote parenthetically in a letter to Harald, "you know I have the bad habit of thinking I can find mistakes in others"). Bohr's innate ability to question and put his finger on fundamental assumptions had already become an important part of his scientist's bag of tools.

Just after submitting his master's thesis, Niels took a holiday to visit a friend, Niels Erik Nørlund, a member of the discussion group that he and Harald had formed. There he met his friend's sister, Margrethe Nørlund, an intelligent, warm young woman with a serene strength and a more than passing interest in science. Niels had met his life partner, and he knew it at once.

As a lifelong friend, Richard Courant, wrote many decades later, after Niels's death, "It was not luck, rather deep insight, which led him to find in young years his wife, who . . . had such a decisive role in making his whole scientific and personal activity possible and harmonious."

Margrethe would become his partner in every way. Their happiness together was always apparent to those who knew them, and their marriage, which would last over 50 years, was unique. As one biographer put it, "Not only by the strength of her great personality and by her knowledge and ability in so many differing fields, but especially by her devotion, Margrethe Bohr became the perfect and indispensable support to her husband."

With the beginning of the school year in the fall of 1909, Harald returned from Göttingen to continue his Ph.D. studies, and the two brothers often studied together. Niels also began work on his doctorate, choosing to continue his work on the electron theory of metals for his thesis.

By January 1910, with Niels still lagging behind, Harald was ready to defend his thesis in mathematics. As is still the case at many universities throughout the world, a candidate for a Ph.D. in Denmark at that time had to answer questions before a faculty committee in defense of the thesis. According to tradition, friends, relatives, and colleagues frequently attended the proceedings in support, and in Harald's case the entire room at the university was packed with a boisterous cheering section composed of his teammates and supporters of his soccer team. If the members of his committee were unsettled by the unusual audience, they showed no sign of it, and Harald passed his candidacy without a hitch, to the joy of the crowd.

For Niels, though, defense of his thesis, on the electron theory of metals, was still more than a year off. Long hours of research and, later, hours of writing once again during a six-week retreat at the vicarage on Fyn lay between him and the moment of victory. In June 1910 he wrote to Harald, "have succeeded only in writing circa fourteen more or less divergent rough drafts." He finally finished that summer, and in August he became engaged to Margrethe Nørlund. But his approaching success—the formal defense of his dissertation the following year—would be marred by the sudden loss of his father.

Christian Bohr had been working late at his laboratory the night of February 2, 1911, after a supper in his home attended by Margrethe Nørlund. He returned home about midnight, when he began to develop sharp chest pains. Recognizing the warning signs of a coronary attack, he called his assistant and family, but the pains subsided. Relieved, he announced that he guessed he would have to give up smoking for a while, but the reprieve was all too short. Moments later he collapsed, a victim of heart failure, just days before his 56th birthday. His remains were cremated and buried in one of Copenhagen's oldest cemeteries near the graves of the physicist Hans Ørsted and the fabulist Hans Christian Andersen.

With the death of Christian Bohr, Niels lost a strong ally, just as he embarked on a career that would have made his philosopher-physiologist father very proud. On May 13, when Niels defended his thesis, the opening page read: "Dedicated with deepest gratitude to the memory of my father."

Niels's introductory remarks at his defense were written in Margrethe Nørlund's handwriting, as most of the rest of his papers would be until he began to find young physicists he could talk into doing the task. Bohr was never a man who thought with pen in hand. He did his best thinking in conversation, pacing about the room, pausing in the middle of sentences and thinking out loud. And, fortunately for science, he was always able to coax willing collaborators into helping him get the words on paper.

On this occasion, however, he was unusually silent.

"Dr. Bohr, a pale and modest young man," reported a newspaper account of the event, "did not take much part in the proceedings, the short duration of which is a record. . . . The words Bohr had written and the questions he had raised were literally so new and unusual that no one was equipped to question them."

That summer, Niels Bohr spent many idyllic hours walking, hiking, and talking with Margrethe and Harald. But as the Nordic days began to shorten in September, he set off for his postgraduate work abroad. Clearly, he would continue his work where the action was: in Cambridge, England, academic home of J. J. Thomson. As he set sail, he may well have been thinking of lines he often quoted from one of his favorite poems by Hans Christian Andersen:

In Denmark I was born, there is my home,
there are my roots, from there my world unfolds . . .

For Niels Bohr was a young man imbued in Danish culture, but who, from the days when he sat listening to learned discussions at his father's knee, reached always outward to embrace the world beyond.

2

Mysteries of the Atom

(1911–1912)

When Bohr arrived in Cambridge in late September 1911, he felt exhilarated. He walked the very paths Isaac Newton and James Clerk Maxwell—two towering geniuses of physics—once had trod, and the days that lay ahead seemed to hold boundless opportunity.

Prior to his death, his father had helped arrange a grant for the young physicist's postgraduate work, to be pursued under the guidance of none other than Joseph John Thomson—"J. J." to the world (his students included)—discoverer of the electron and head of the prestigious Cavendish Laboratory. Niels lost no time making contact. As soon as he had found a place to live and done the minimal unpacking, he set off to see J. J., with a translation of his own Ph.D. dissertation into English (done, rather badly, by a friend) and a copy of one of J. J.'s recent papers under his arm.

J. J. Thomson, who discovered the electron, invited Bohr to come to England to study at Cambridge University.
(Original portrait by Arthur Hacker, A. R. A., courtesy AIP Emilio Segrè Visual Archives)

J. J., who was 56 at the time, had already been head of the Cavendish for 27 years—having taken the place of Lord Rayleigh at the age of 28. He was only the third head of the prestigious laboratory—the first director had been James Clerk Maxwell. Thomson was an intense-looking man who wore wire-rimmed glasses and a slightly drooping mustache. His hair, a bit long, swept across the crown, and his proper tweed coat and winged collar tended to look disheveled, the requisite tie and cuff links in place but, like his cluttered desk, not necessarily in order. But, for all his erudition and fame—he had won the Nobel Prize only five years earlier for his work on the electron and was knighted in 1908—his manner was genuinely warm and sociable. As Niels Bohr made his way along the darkly paneled halls of the Cavendish Laboratory and entered Thomson's

Interlude in Cambridge

During his leisure hours in Cambridge, Niels called on former students of his father's, attended teas and gatherings sponsored by the ladies of the English academic community, read the works of Charles Dickens with dictionary in hand to improve his English (remembering the Dickens stories his father used to read when he was a boy), and enjoyed long walks through the countryside.

After one of these autumn excursions, he wrote enthusiastically to Margrethe, ". . . and then I went on the loveliest walk for an hour before dinner across most beautiful meadows along the river, with the hedges flecked with red berries and with isolated wind-blown willow-trees—just imagine all this under the most magnificent autumn sky with scurrying clouds and blustering wind . . ."

Always athletic, Bohr also joined a soccer club and, as the weather got colder, enjoyed ice skating. Harald came for a visit at Christmas.

But as far as physics went, Bohr spent his time working on a lusterless project on cathode ray production, suggested by Thomson. It was not going well and seemed to hold little promise of yielding fruitful results. Try as he might to sound upbeat in his letters, he became restless. No one he knew in England understood Danish, and Bohr's usual roundabout way of speaking and his soft voice didn't help office, he might have been overcome with a sense of awe, had it not been for his new mentor's disarmingly friendly manner.

Criticizing the Great J. J.

Young Bohr's English was halting, but he began by opening Thomson's paper and pointing out a few places where he thought Thomson had possibly gone wrong. Bohr finished by offering Thomson his dissertation on the application of electron theory to metals. He hoped that Thomson might read the thesis and discuss it with him. Perhaps he even might be willing to help Bohr get it published in England. Thomson accepted the dissertation cordially and placed it on top of a stack of papers on his desk.

his less-than-complete command of English. His colleagues couldn't understand, for example, what he meant by "loaded" electrons (he meant "charged"), and his miscommunications were often comical. On other occasions the handicap must have been very frustrating. In one instance, at a meeting, Thomson waved aside comments by Bohr as useless, only to restate the same ideas in different words.

Finally Bohr could stand the suspense no longer, and he went again to visit Thomson. The interview was again cordial, but the dissertation remained unread, still in a stack on the director's desk. Unknown to Bohr, Thomson was notorious for neglecting student papers and correspondence. Also, Thomson never said so, but his lack of interest may have grown out of the fact that since completing his own work on electron theory, he had turned to other subjects and was no longer as involved as he once was. The fact is, he never did read Niels Bohr's dissertation, which would not be published in a good English translation until 1972.

Bohr left the director's office deeply discouraged. Things were not going so well at Cambridge after all. Years later he would comment, "The whole thing was very interesting in Cambridge but it was absolutely useless."

Bohr went back to his rooms elated. That evening he wrote to his brother:

29 Sept. 1911
Eltisley Avenue 10,
Newnham, Cambridge

Oh Harald!
Things are going so well for me. I have just been talking to J. J. Thomson and have explained to him, as well as I could, my ideas about radiation, magnetism, etc. If you only knew what it meant to me to talk to such a man. He was extremely nice to me, and we talked about so much; and I do believe that he thought there was some sense in what I said. He is now going to read [my dissertation] and he invited me to have dinner with him Sunday at Trinity College; then he will talk with me about it. You can imagine that I am happy. . . . I now have my own little flat. It is at the edge of town and is very nice in all respects. I have two rooms and eat all alone in my own room. It is very nice here; now, as I am sitting and writing to you, it blazes and rumbles in my own little fireplace.

However, time passed, and Bohr heard no word from Thomson. Had he perhaps gone too far, calling the great physicist's theory into question? He wrote to Margrethe, "I wonder what he will say to my disagreement with his ideas." A few weeks later he wrote her again: "I'm longing to hear what Thomson will say. He's a great man. I hope he will not get angry with my silly talk."

Bohr was not about to let his one year in England go so badly. He resolved to make a change, and he looked toward Manchester, which may have seemed an unlikely choice—compared to Cambridge, the University of Manchester was like meat and potatoes next to caviar and wine. But for a student of physics, Manchester had one great asset: Ernest Rutherford.

Rutherford and the Story So Far

Rutherford was an exuberant man with big hands, a big walrus mustache, and a booming voice. When Ernest Rutherford had arrived on scholarship at the Cavendish Laboratory from his native New Zealand, he was a brash 24-year-old with strong opinions, plenty of ambition, and no money. He also had the qualities of a fine physics experimentalist, which Thomson recognized immediately.

Rutherford could not have arrived at a better time. Three months later Röntgen discovered the X-ray; three months after that Becquerel discovered radioactivity. And a year later Thomson discovered the electron. By this time Rutherford was working in Thomson's lab on questions surrounding radioactivity.

In 1898, when Marie Curie reported her discovery of new radioactive substances, one of them, radium, proved to be several million times more radioactive than Becquerel's uranium salts. Physicists and chemists became intensely interested in the subject, and Rutherford was in on the ground floor. In his work with J. J., he had learned just the right techniques for discovering more about radioactivity, and he began studying rays emitted by uranium. What he was trying to do was dissect the atom. In the process he found out something big: Uranium gave off two very distinct types of radiation. He called one "alpha" radiation (after the first letter of the Greek alphabet). Alpha rays were easily absorbed by matter. The other he called "beta" radiation (after the second letter of the Greek alphabet). This was a far more penetrating ray. (Paul U. Villard from France discovered a third even more penetrating ray in 1900, which was later named "gamma" by Rutherford, after the third letter of the Greek alphabet.)

Australian physicist Ernest Rutherford, at the University of Manchester at the time of Bohr's arrival in England, was an experimental physicist with a strong reputation. He and Bohr, with his theoretical insights, made a good team. (Library of Congress)

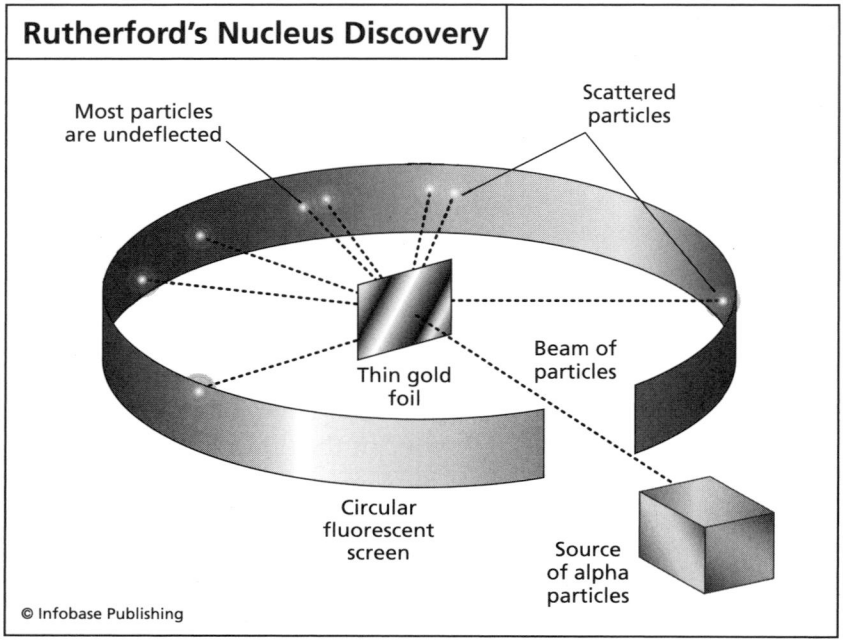

This diagram depicts Rutherford's discovery of the nucleus of an atom.

The competition was keen, as Rutherford wrote home to his mother: "Among so many scientific bugs knocking about, one has a little difficulty in rising to the front." But Rutherford was never one to let anything, much less a little competition, stop him. In later years his students nicknamed him "the Crocodile" because, as one explained, "the crocodile cannot turn its head . . . it must always go forward with all devouring jaws." He was tireless in every quest and loved his role as one who put endless questions to nature. His great success, as Bohr would later say, came from his knack of forming questions in such a way that they could produce the most useful answers.

A consummate experimentalist, Rutherford generally had little use for theorists. "They play games with their symbols," he said, "but we [experimentalists] must turn out the real facts of Nature." He had a particular talent for experimental design and an uncanny ability to pick out one significant fact from a mass of confusing detail. As one colleague remarked, "With one movement from afar, Rutherford so to speak threaded the needle the first time."

Rutherford completed this early work on alpha and beta radiation at the Cavendish, but by the time it was published in 1899, he had accepted an appointment as professor of physics at McGill University in Canada. There, in 1900, he noticed that thorium gave off a radioactive gas, and he enlisted the help of a young chemistry professor, Frederick Soddy, to help him identify the gas. When Soddy examined it, he found that the gas had no chemical properties at all. Only one element fit that description, the chemically inert gas argon. From this evidence, according to Soddy, they reached "the tremendous and inevitable conclusion that the element thorium was slowly and spontaneously transmuting itself into argon gas!" Rutherford and Soddy had discovered the stunning fact that, through radiation, radioactive elements change themselves into other elements.

In the following years, Rutherford continued to unravel the threads of the complex mysteries surrounding the transmutation of the radioactive elements. This work done at McGill University earned him, in 1908, a Nobel Prize, oddly enough, not in physics but in chemistry.

By 1908 Rutherford had returned to England, having accepted the position as professor of experimental physics at the University of Manchester that he held four years later, when Bohr arrived. At Manchester, his students tended to be mature, and most of them already held degrees. One of them, a young German physicist named Hans Geiger, teamed up with Rutherford, and together they began bombarding thin pieces of gold foil with alpha particles. Most of the alpha bombarders passed right through the foil, which was exactly what the experimenters expected, based on Thomson's "plum pudding" model of the atom. But some of the alpha particles struck the gold foil and were deflected at a sharp angle—often 90 degrees or more! This amazed Rutherford, who remarked, "It was almost as incredible as if you fired a 15-inch shell at a piece of tissue paper and it came back and hit you." The Thomson model of the atom clearly required rethinking.

Doing Physics in Manchester

Early in 1911 Rutherford came buoyantly to Geiger. "I know what the atom looks like!" he exclaimed. Based on his results, Rutherford put

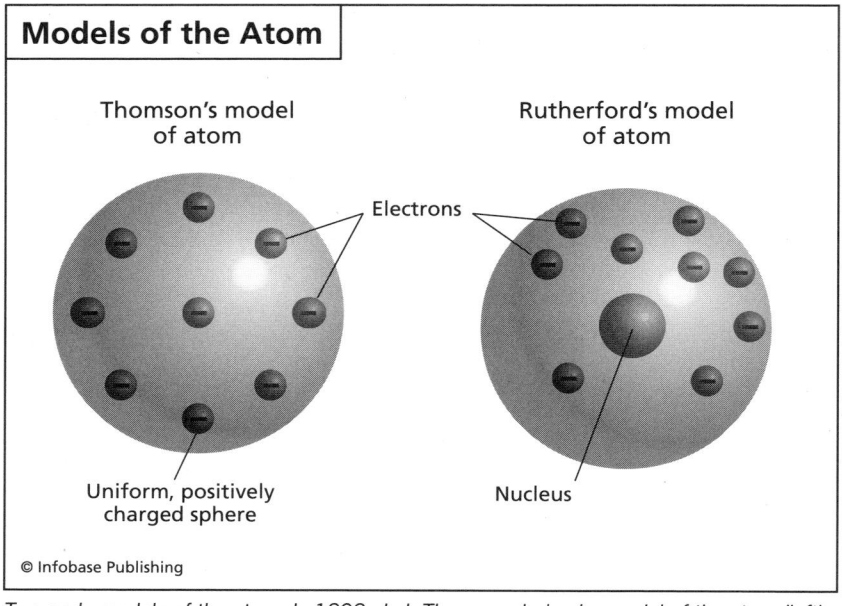

Two early models of the atom. In 1898, J. J. Thomson derived a model of the atom (left) based on his discovery of the electron. He asserted that atoms were spheres of positively charged matter with negatively charged electrons embedded in them—something like raisins in pound cake. In 1911, Ernest Rutherford came up with the idea that each atom consisted of a tiny positive nucleus (right) with electrons circling somewhere outside it.

together a new idea of the atom: What if all the positively charged particles in the atom were not spread like a fluid throughout the atom, but lumped together in the center in one tiny core area? This "nucleus" (a term he came up with in 1912) was thousands of times heavier than an electron, so most of the atom's mass would be contained there, composed of positively charged particles. An equal number of negatively charged electrons would be found in motion somewhere outside the nucleus. The rest of the atom would be empty space. If the nucleus was the size of a marble, sitting in the center of the field in an empty football stadium, its electrons would be perched on the outer walls of the stadium. It was a compelling idea—a sort of tiny planetary system that mirrored the larger solar system we live in. In the bombardment experiments, most of the bombarding alpha particles would pass straight through the comparatively vast areas of empty space. But a few would hit the nucleus of positively charged particles, be repelled (since alpha particles are also positive) and bounce back.

Rutherford's discovery of the atomic nucleus was stunning, and it would ultimately earn him the title of "the Newton of atomic physics." But not many people paid much attention to it at the time. In fact, in the fall of 1911, Rutherford attended an international conference of the world's leading physicists, the first of a series of prestigious conferences known as the Solvay conferences (after the man who organized the first one). And at that conference he made no mention of his new atomic model.

When Bohr arrived in Cambridge, however, he already knew about Rutherford's work with radioactivity from the journals he had read and about his emerging new model of the atom, which Bohr considered to be at the cutting edge of physics. (Of course, not everyone, least of all Thomson, agreed.) Now Bohr thought that perhaps it was time for a visit to Manchester. He arranged to see an old friend of his father's there who was also acquainted with Ernest Rutherford. In this way Bohr got to meet Rutherford, and the two hit it off immediately.

Bohr saw Rutherford again a few weeks later at the December 8, 1911, Cavendish Research Students' Annual Dinner. As one of J. J.'s "old students," Rutherford was invited to give a speech. The mood was jolly and the menu was posh—including turbot, shrimp, plover, mutton, turkey, pheasant, and plum pudding—no doubt with raisins. The program included rollicking limericks sung with more gusto than art, including "My name is J. J. Thomson and my lab's in Free School Lane/There's no professor like J. J. my students all maintain" and "For an alpha ray/Is a thing to pay/And a Nobel Prize/One cannot despise/And Rutherford/Has greatly scored/As all the world now recognize."

Rutherford spoke enthusiastically and excitedly, and Bohr was impressed with the charm, power, and enthusiasm with which he described the work of C. T. R. Wilson, an experimentalist who had invented an instrument known as a cloud chamber, used for tracking atomic particles. With his cloud chamber, Wilson could see the paths of charged particles visible as lines of water droplets hovering in a supersaturated fog. He had just photographed the evidence of alpha particles in his cloud chamber as they scattered from interactions with nuclei, showing scatterings very similar to those that had preceded Rutherford's discovery of the nucleus just a few months before.

Sometime shortly thereafter, having consulted with Harald during his Christmas visit, Bohr made arrangements with Rutherford to transfer to Manchester to finish his year. Rutherford welcomed the idea, although he advised the eager young scientist to finish out his work with Thomson first. This Bohr did, explaining to Thomson that he "should be glad to know something about radioactivity," and then he set off for Manchester in March 1912.

Teamwork: Rutherford and Bohr

Niels Bohr was perhaps the only theorist ever to hit it off with Rutherford. "Bohr's different" was the explanation Rutherford offered in his usual brusque way. "He's a football player." In a way that quick summary represented something important about Bohr as a physicist: He was in every way a man who lived in the real world. He prided himself on the literal-mindedness that helped him maintain his connection with the physical world while he thought about the ideas of physics.

But Bohr and Rutherford were a strange pair, Rutherford brash and exuberant, Bohr speaking not much above a whisper, digging in his mind for the perfect word and, in the words of fellow physicist C. P. Snow, "on not finding it, . . . pauses, minutes long, in which he reiterated a word which was clinging to his mind." The contrasts between these two men and their problem-solving methods epitomized the differing styles of experimental and theoretical physicists that emerged fully in the first decades of the century—no two people better typified the dichotomy than Bohr and Rutherford. Bohr the ruminator, with enormous powers of concentration, thought things through as he talked and frequently would hit upon an idea spontaneously in the middle of a conversation. He had no mechanical talent, however, for coaxing resistant laboratory apparatus into smooth operation and exhaustive experimentation. Rutherford, by contrast, had the intractable persistence needed to pursue a course of action and see it through to its outcome, but lacked Bohr's ability to daydream with purpose. In solving the "serious problems of physics," the physicist Otto Frisch would later recall that Bohr "moved with the skill of a spider in apparently empty space, judging accurately how much weight each slender thread of argument could bear."

For Bohr, Manchester was a wonderful contrast to Cambridge. Granted, it was not such a pretty place. The bustling industrial city was noisy, its buildings blackened and sooty from the belching factory smokestacks. Horse-drawn drays crowded the busy, cobblestone streets. But the physics laboratory at the university was rapidly becoming one of the most productive in the world. And, at its head, Rutherford created around himself an atmosphere of intellectual excitement and openness in which young Bohr flourished—and found the seeds for his own teaching style in later years. One of Rutherford's collaborators, E. Andrade, once wrote this description of his style: "Although there was no doubt as to who was the boss, everybody said what he liked without constraint . . . He was always full of fire and infectious enthusiasm when describing work into which he had put his heart and always generous in his acknowledgement of the work of others."

In Manchester, a young Hungarian Bohr's age, Georg von Hevesy, took Bohr under his wing and introduced him to the life of the lab. Hevesy had followed Rutherford to Manchester from McGill the year before and was working on a project—proposed by Rutherford—to separate radioactive decay products from their parent substances. It turned out to be an extremely difficult challenge, one that gave Hevesy another idea. Over the next several decades he developed the science of using radioactive tracers in medical and biological research. Hevesy became a good friend of Bohr's, and he also had an extensive knowledge of chemistry—especially radiochemistry—which turned out to be exactly what Bohr needed for the work ahead.

Bohr began by taking an eight-week laboratory course, with Geiger as one of the instructors, in the experimental methods of radioactive research. The course ended May 3. After that, Rutherford set him to work studying the absorption of alpha particles in aluminum. Bohr wrote to his brother, ". . . Rutherford is a man you can rely on; he comes regularly and enquires how things are going and talks about the smallest details. . . . Rutherford is such an outstanding man and really interested in the work of all the people who are around him. . . ."

Exploring Atomic Structure

The equipment was primitive by modern standards, and the work was tedious, but there was always a sense of discovery in the air. Geiger once described it as "the gloomy cellar," which Rutherford had fitted with the delicate apparatus he used for the study of the alpha rays. "Rutherford loved this room," wrote Geiger. "One went down two steps and then heard from the darkness Rutherford's voice reminding one that a hot-pipe crossed the room at head-level, and to step over two water-pipes. Then finally, in the feeble light one saw the great man himself seated at his apparatus."

Each afternoon in the lab, work was set aside for tea. Rutherford would come in, sit down, and talk. The lab group avidly discussed politics and sports and, of course, work. Ideas always were exchanged freely at these daily get-togethers. So much was happening in physics that no one was afraid that someone else would take his idea and publish it first. There were plenty of vital topics for everyone.

Outside the Manchester lab, though, not many scientists had made much of Rutherford's discovery of the nuclear atom, partly because Rutherford himself had not made a strong case for it.

During this period, Bohr began thinking about some of what he had learned at Manchester. Hevesy mentioned to him that the number of radioactive elements far outnumbered the available spaces on the periodic table. Bohr remembered that, according to Soddy, most radioactive elements were not new elements, just variants of natural elements that were already known. (Soddy later came up with the name "isotopes," the term now used for such variants.) For example, uranium 235, which is radioactive and very rare, is an isotope of uranium 238. Bohr realized that the natural elements should be organized in the periodic table not as they had been, according to the weight of an element (its atomic weight) but according to the number of protons in its nucleus (its atomic number)—and that the atomic number for the radioelements must be the same as the natural elements with which they were chemically identical. From

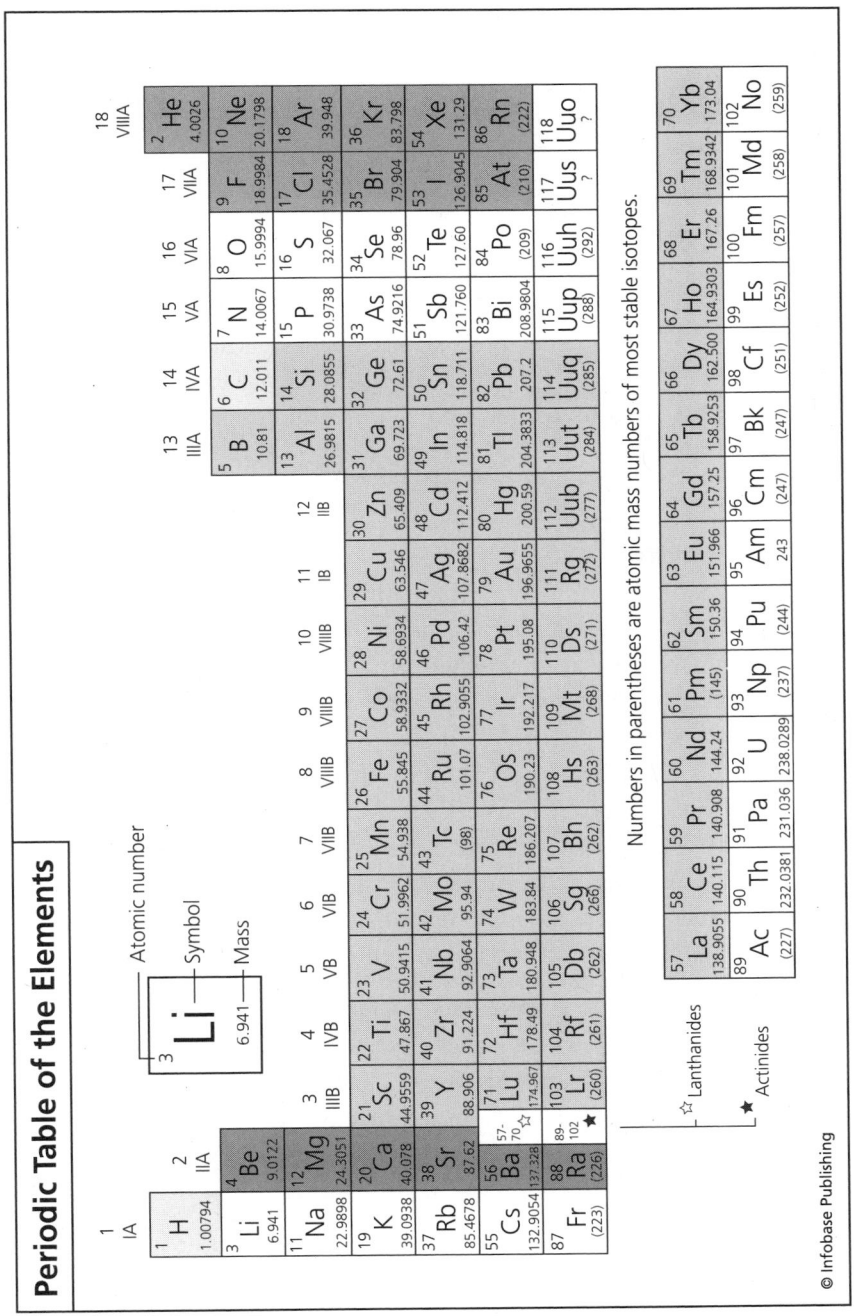

The periodic table of the elements provides a scheme for organizing the elements and their attributes in an easily referenced display.

these ideas, he roughed out what is now known as the radioactive displacement law. Basically, this law states that when an element emits an alpha particle (a helium nucleus, having the atomic number 2) through radioactive decay, it moves two places to the left on the periodic table (down in atomic number); when it emits a beta particle, it moves to the right one place (up in atomic number because, as an energetic electron, the beta particle leaves behind an extra positive charge in the nucleus).

Bohr was excited when he had worked out his calculations, and he ran to report to Rutherford. To his surprise, Rutherford was cautious. Bohr later recalled, "Rutherford . . . thought that the meager evidence [obtained up to that point] about the nuclear atom was not certain enough to draw such consequences. And I said to him that I was sure that it would be the final proof of his atom." As it turned out later, Bohr was right, but because of Rutherford's caution, he didn't publish his ideas.

However, as Bohr was waiting for some radium he needed for another alpha-scattering experiment, he came across a paper on the energy loss that occurs when alpha particles are not scattered by a collision with a nucleus but pass through a metal instead (as the vast majority of them do). It was written by another student of Rutherford's, Charles Galton Darwin, the grandson of the great evolutionist Charles Robert Darwin. Darwin had figured, correctly, that most of the energy loss was caused by encounters the alpha particles made with electrons. But he hadn't considered how or even whether the electrons might be moving. Instead, he assumed that the electrons were free. As Niels wrote to Harald, concerning Darwin's paper:

> *It seemed to me that it was not only not quite right mathematically (this was however rather trifling) but quite unsatisfactory in its basic conception . . . I have worked out a theory about it, which, however modest, may perhaps throw some light upon a few things concerning the structure of atoms. . . . I am considering publishing a little paper about it.*

Bohr began his paper but didn't finish it until after he had returned to Denmark, partly because he found some other ideas to think about that were more exciting. By mid-June 1912, he had worked out some more calculations and went to see Rutherford again. In a letter to Harald dated June 19, Bohr reported what happened:

> *It could be that I've perhaps found out a little bit about the structure of atoms. You must not tell anyone anything about it, otherwise I certainly could not write you this soon. If I'm right, it would not be an indication of the nature of a possibility . . . but perhaps a little piece of reality. . . . You understand that I may yet be wrong, for it hasn't been worked out fully yet (but I don't think so); nor do I believe that Rutherford thinks it's completely wild; he is the right kind of man and would never say that he was convinced of something that was not entirely worked out. You can imagine how anxious I am to finish quickly.*

Bohr had found himself drawn to questions surrounding the Rutherford model of the atom. There was something wrong with this atomic model based on the discovery of the nucleus, the model that depicted the atom as a miniature solar system.

As Rutherford had pointed out, the electron was attracted to the opposite electrical charge of the nucleus—the electron having a negative charge, the nucleus a positive charge. This explained why, as the positively charged alpha particles sped toward the nucleus, they had veered away so dramatically—because like charges repel.

In this configuration, an electron would move in an elliptical orbit around the nucleus, in the same way that the planets move around the Sun. But the idea of a moving electron seemed impossible—impossible because, according to the laws of electricity, a moving charge must produce electromagnetic radiation (light, for example). If all electrons produced radiation, then all matter would radiate, which it doesn't. An even bigger problem lay in the fact that as radiation is released by moving electrons, they should lose energy and rapidly spiral into the nucleus. The principle is similar to the way a satellite losing energy from the drag of the Earth's atmosphere will eventually crash into the Earth. But Rutherford's electrons would crash into the nucleus in as little as one 10-billionth of a second. Atoms, according to Rutherford's model, in short, must be very unstable. But, of course, atoms are not unstable. This was the dilemma that Bohr undertook to solve, and he believed he had an answer.

He went back to his rooms to continue his calculations, but he was running out of time. His departure from Manchester was planned for the end of July and he was eagerly awaited in Denmark, where he was planning to marry Margrethe Nørlund on August 1. On July 17 he wrote Harald again:

> *I believe I have found out a few things; but it is certainly taking more time to work them out than I was foolish enough to believe at first. I hope to have a little paper ready to show to Rutherford before I leave, so I'm busy, so busy; but the unbelievable heat here in Manchester doesn't exactly help my diligence. How I look forward to talking to you!*

Five days later Bohr had shown his paper to Rutherford and received hearty encouragement to continue. He left Manchester July 24, 1912, his postdoctoral year concluded. His work, however, had only just begun. As he headed home to Denmark, his thoughts turned to a future filled with even greater possibilities than when he had arrived in England the year before.

3

Birth of Bohr's Atom

(1913–1924)

In the town of Slagelse, about 50 miles southwest of Copenhagen on the island of Sjaelland, Niels Bohr and Margrethe Nørlund were married in a civil ceremony at the town hall on August 1, 1912.

Niels had quietly resigned his membership in the Lutheran Church the previous April. Although he had sought out religion as a child, by the time of their marriage he no longer "was taken" by it, as he put it. "And for me it was exactly the same," Margrethe later explained. "[Interest in religion] disappeared completely," although at the time of their wedding, she was still a member of the Lutheran Church. (Niels's parents were also married in a civil, not a religious, ceremony, and Harald also resigned his membership in the Lutheran Church just before his wedding, a few years later.)

Flags lined the streets of the town on the day of their wedding, and the Nørlunds had made many preparations for a gala celebration, but the ceremony itself was only two minutes long, performed by the chief of police, before members of the immediate family. Harald was the best man. When Niels heard that Margrethe's mother had planned a three-hour wedding dinner, he exclaimed, "How is it really possible to take three hours for a dinner? Can't we take the ferry at 7:00?"

The ferry Niels was so eager to catch would cross the Store Baelt from the island of Sjaelland to the Danish mainland to start the new couple out on the first leg of their honeymoon trip to England, where they stopped off in Cambridge. There Bohr completed his paper on the absorption of alpha particles. When he reached Manchester on August 12, he handed Rutherford his manuscript for publication in *Philosophical Magazine.* In Manchester, Margrethe met Ernest and Mary Rutherford, who were nearly as enchanted by her as Niels was, delighted that he had found someone so perfectly his match. The four became great friends.

Margrethe and Niels returned to Denmark in September, where they settled into their new life together in Copenhagen. Bohr carried the whirlwind style of his childhood and youth into his adult years. As he had written to Harald from Manchester, "I have so many things that I should like to try . . ." One longtime friend, Jens Rud Nielsen, looking back on that period from 1912 to 1913, recalled, "He would come into the yard, pushing his bicycle, faster than anybody else. He was an incessant worker and seemed always to be in a hurry."

As far as prospects for an academic career were concerned, Bohr clearly realized that, even with a fine record, he had to apply considerable energy if he hoped to have any position at all in his homeland, in a field as esoteric as physics. Denmark, after all, was a small country, and at that time the University of Copenhagen was its only university. Only one professorship in physics existed, and that one wasn't open.

Fortunately, he had thought ahead, knowing he might need several tries to get his foot in the door. Shortly after he received his doctorate, in the summer of 1911, he applied for a docentship (a much lower paid position) in physics. He was turned down. Then, during his stay in England, he heard that his former professor, Christian Christiansen, was resigning, effective August 31, 1912. Bohr applied, even though he knew that the position was much more likely to go to Martin Knudsen, a docent who had far greater seniority. Again Bohr was turned down. Knudsen received the appointment and recommended his own assistant as docent. Now Knudsen's professorial position would not be open for many years—until 1941, as it turned out—and the docentship he vacated was also filled. However, Knudsen offered Bohr a teaching assistantship beginning in the fall of 1912, which Bohr accepted. It was not his first, or even second, choice, but it was a start.

The Black Body Dilemma

Meanwhile, Bohr turned his attention back to the problems that had so intrigued him just before the end of his postdoctoral year: the dilemma of Rutherford's atomic model.

As early as his doctoral dissertation, Bohr had recognized, as he put it, that "One must assume that there are forces in nature of a kind completely different from the usual mechanical sort." By "the usual mechanical sort," he meant forces that classical physics had talked about since the time of Galileo and Newton. In classical terms, energy and matter can be thought of as moving along a ramp, in continuous gradations, with a clear relationship between cause and effect. But very recently, different forces had come to the attention of physicists through the work of two men, Max Planck and Albert Einstein. Their ideas were the stuff of which revolutions are made.

Max Planck did not seem like the revolutionary type, though. Tall and spare, quiet and dignified, even a bit stuffy and pedantic, he was completely devoted to tradition and authority, both in his physics and in his life. Born in Kiel, Germany in 1858, Planck had specialized in thermodynamics, and he secured an appointment at the University of Berlin in 1889. In general, he appeared to travel pretty much on the beaten path. In fact, when he first started his scientific work in college, one of his professors warned him against pursuing physics. The field, he said, was heading for a dead end. All the great work had already been done, leaving only a few minor details to clear up. But Max Planck was a detail man.

It so happened that one of the "minor details" left to tidy up in the field of thermodynamics was known as the ultraviolet catastrophe, a name dramatic enough to attract anyone's attention. It was the result of problems involved in trying to understand a phenomenon known as black body radiation.

A black body, in physics, is one that absorbs all frequencies of light—something like a piece of coal, only blacker. However, any object with a temperature higher than the temperature of its surroundings loses heat by radiation (the emission of waves or particles through substances). The hotter the object, the more radiation it produces. Logically, since a black body absorbs all frequencies, it should, when heated, radiate all frequencies equally. But that does not happen. Instead, black bodies emit larger quantities of some wavelengths than others. When physicists tried to explain these results quantitatively, they came up with an equation that seemed to work well except that it predicted an infinite amount of radiation at the ultraviolet end of the spectrum, which would be impossible, according to the laws of physics. No one could come up with a way to resolve the dilemma in terms of the current physical theory of the 1890s, although several people certainly had tried.

Beginning in 1897, Planck spent the next three years of his life trying to find a solution to this problem. Finally he came up with an idea just before a meeting of the Berlin Physical Society on October 19, 1900. He announced his finding there, and that night colleagues from the meeting rushed to compare the figures to the values found in experiments. They matched—which was very exciting news.

What Planck had proposed was that energy is not infinitely indivisible. Like matter, he said, energy exists not in a continuum, but in discrete, tiny particles or packets. In other words, Planck solved the black body radiation problem by proposing that vibrating particles can radiate only at certain energies—not on a continuum, as classical physics would expect. He said the permitted values could be found by applying a constant, "a universal constant," he said, "which I called *h*. Since it had the dimension of action (energy × time), I gave it the name, *elementary quantum of action.*" (He used the Latin word *quantum,* an adjective meaning "how much," to describe this new discrete quantity. "Quanta" is the plural form.) In radiation, he maintained, only discrete energies could appear, limited to whole-number multiples of $h\nu$; that is, the frequency (ν) times Planck's new constant, *h*. Today this universal constant is known as Planck's constant. Planck calculated it to be a very small number and came amazingly close to the modern calculated value of 6.63 times 10^{-27}

erg-seconds. Today Planck's constant is recognized as one of the fundamental constants of the universe.

Because the size of these quanta was in direct proportion to the frequency, radiation at low frequencies requires only small packets or quanta of energy. But, for a frequency twice as high, radiation would require twice the amount of energy.

Following Planck's idea that energy can be emitted only in whole quanta, it becomes very easy for a body to radiate at low frequencies—not that much energy has to be pulled together to make up a quantum of energy. But at high frequencies, pulling a quantum's-worth of energy together is not so easy. The quantum-energy requirements to radiate at the high-frequency end of the spectrum are so great that it's very unlikely to happen. So black bodies do not radiate all frequencies equally, and that's the key to the "ultraviolet catastrophe."

Conservative Max Planck had no heart for pushing this idea to its natural, radical conclusions, but another, younger physicist made use of Planck's theory in a paper, published in 1905, that would win him the Nobel Prize in physics in 1921. That young physicist was Albert Einstein.

If Max Planck was noted for his middle-class conservatism, Albert Einstein was the epitome of the complete rebel, a loner who preferred to work alone, a wanderer in the highest realms of thought, uncomfortable with and often disdainful of the everyday preoccupations of the average man or woman. As he once explained, he sought out science to get away from the "I" and the "we." He preferred to think instead about the "it." Supremely confident of his own genius, like his greatest predecessor, Isaac Newton, Einstein walked his own way, to his own challenges, and worried little about what he called "the chains of the merely personal . . . dominated by wishes, hopes, and primitive feelings."

By 1905, at the age of 26, he had produced no fewer than five papers, all of which were published that year by the German *Yearbook of Physics.* In the first he examined a topic that would ultimately win him the Nobel Prize. In the second, he introduced what would later be called the special theory of relativity, one of his two most famous contributions to physics. In the special theory of relativity, Einstein established his famous formula $E=mc^2$, where E is energy, m is mass, and c represents the speed of light, which is always constant. This formula showed the interrelationship of mass and energy, and by using it, Einstein could show that the laws of physics are the same in all reference frames that are moving at constant velocities relative to one another. (He later succeeded in applying his theory of relativity to the more general case of accelerated systems, establishing a new theory of gravitation of which Newton's classic theory was a special case. The general theory of relativity, published in 1915, held enormous implications for understanding how the universe works.) In a third paper published in 1905, he examined an aspect of statistical mechanics and Brownian motion, the apparently erratic movement of pollen in fluids. Another two explored further aspects of special theory of relativity and Brownian motion.

But his Nobel-prize-winning work dealt with a mysterious phenomenon known as the photoelectric effect, that is, the fact that when light falls on certain metals, electrons are emitted. (It is the principle that makes solar arrays on satellites and spacecraft work.) But, strangely, there is no connection between the brightness of the light and its ability to knock electrons free of the metal. Instead, it is the *color* of the light that matters—its frequency. No one had been able to explain this mystifying fact. Classical physics—that is, explanations based on what Bohr would call "forces in nature of the usual mechanical sort"—could offer no explanation.

Using Quantum Physics

That is where Einstein stepped in, making use of Planck's quantum theory, which had been gathering dust for a couple of years without too much attention. Einstein pointed out that a particular wavelength of light is made up of quanta of fixed energy content, according to quantum theory. When a quantum of energy bombards an atom of a metal, the atom releases an electron of fixed energy content and no other. A brighter light would contain more quanta, still always of fixed energy content, causing the emission of more electrons, also still all of the same energy content. When the light's wavelength is shorter (and the frequency higher), more energy is contained in the quanta and the electrons released are more energetic. Very long wavelengths (of lower frequency) would be made up of quanta having much smaller energy content, in some cases too small to cause any electrons to be released. And this threshold would vary depending on the metal.

Once again Planck's theory had succeeded in explaining a physical phenomenon where classical physics could not. It was the first major step in establishing what would become known as quantum mechanics, the recognition of the discrete and discontinuous nature of all matter, especially noticeable on the scale of the very small.

Bohr's great insight was to see how the theory of the quantum could be used to explain how things work within the structure of atoms and their particles—specifically to overcome the problem of mechanical instability in Rutherford's model. As he left Manchester in July, he had already arrived at the kernel of his thinking, namely that since classical mechanics predicted instability where there clearly was none, he would call on the quantum approach to describe what actually occurred. Planck had first introduced quantum principles to explain what could not be explained classically in thermodynamics. Einstein had done the same for light. Now Bohr planned to test out quantum principles as a way of explaining what went on within the atom itself.

Once back in Denmark, Bohr worked on these ideas all during the fall and early winter months of 1912. First, he assumed that electrons could not orbit an atom's nucleus willy-nilly in just any orbit. He proposed that "stationary states," as he called them, must exist in the atom—specific orbits that electrons could occupy without spiraling inward and crashing into the nucleus. When he figured the numbers for his model, he found that they coincided with several experimental results. When scientists see this sort of coincidence—as Max Planck's colleagues also had—they recognize that it can be an indication that they are heading down the right path. Of course, it also can be sheer coincidence. What bothered Bohr about his model was that it was arbitrary. It explained some chemical phenomena, but it seemed no more real than Thomson's plum pudding model.

The Story of Spectra

Then Bohr happened to come across a series of papers by J. W. Nicholson, a professor of mathematics at King's College, London.

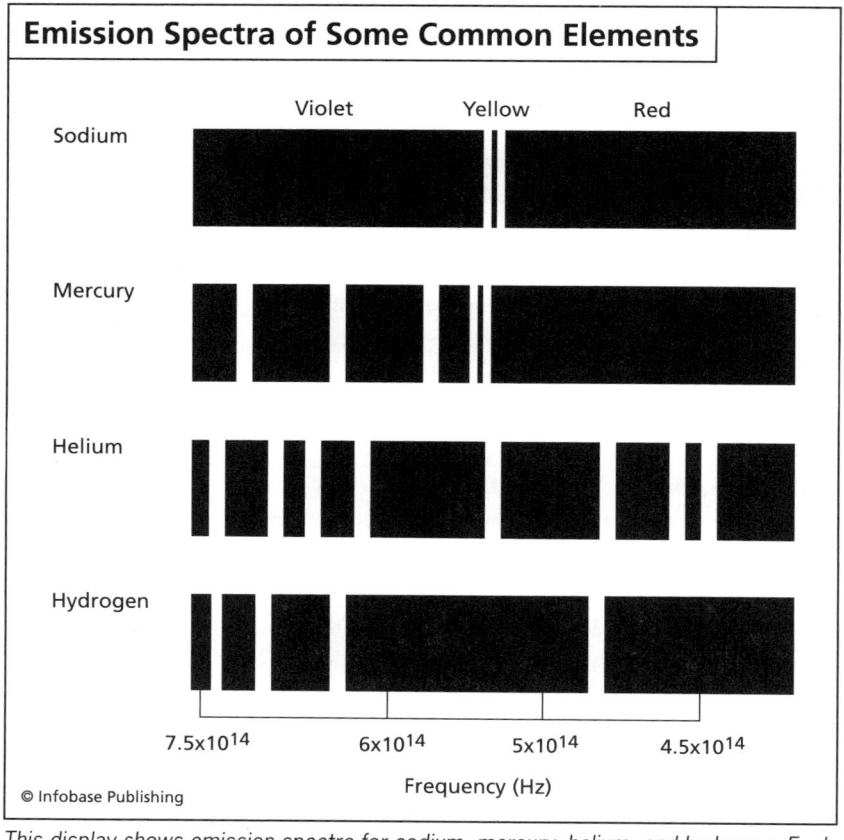

This display shows emission spectra for sodium, mercury, helium, and hydrogen. Each element displays a unique discrete spectrum, an identity marker almost like a fingerprint. This fact puzzled scientists for years until Bohr came up with his model of the atom. Bohr suggested that electrons release energy only while making jumps from one orbit to another (explaining the discrete spectral lines emitted by the elements). He surmised that the electrons move only in certain allowed orbits at specific distances from the nucleus of each element.

Bohr had met Nicholson and did not think much of his abilities, but what startled him was that Nicholson had proposed an explanation for an unusual spectrum in the corona of the Sun by suggesting a model of the atom that used quantum principles. Nicholson had made mistakes, but Bohr began to worry about competition. He had hold of such an exciting idea, and he hoped he would have time to work it out in detail and publish before someone else got there. So Nicholson's paper threw more fuel on an already intensely burning flame. More important, however, Nicholson's introduction of spectra into the picture gave Bohr an idea.

He had not even considered the idea that the spectra produced by the elements might be related to his problem. In the last interview he gave, he said, "The spectra was a very difficult problem. . . . One thought that this is marvelous, but it is not possible to make progress there. Just as if you have the wing of a butterfly, then certainly it is very regular with the colors and so on, but nobody thought that one could get the basis of biology from the coloring of the wing of a butterfly." And so, who would think that the coloring of spectra would have anything to do with the basis of physics?

In the 19th century, physicists had discovered that each element produces a characteristic spectrum of light when heated. Sodium, for instance, emits light only at particular wavelengths—yellow, in this case. Potassium emits a violet light. And so on. In terms of Planck's theorem, that meant that the atoms of each element produce light quanta only of a particular energy. Physicists

What Are Spectra?

When a radiating material (such as a glowing, low-density gas) emits energy, it can be identified by the unique pattern of light emitted in a very small range of wavelengths (or frequencies) in the electromagnetic spectrum. The pattern of several emission lines is characteristic of the gas and is called the emission spectrum. To the surprise of scientists investigating this phenomenon in the early 1800s, they found that each radiating substance has a unique, characteristic emission spectrum. A continuous spectrum may appear in cases where a smooth distribution of various light forms such as white light. When individual atoms of the same substance emit heat a line spectrum appears. During his Nobel–winning theoretical work, when Bohr figured out how the structure of an atom worked, he finally understood why hydrogen emits a single line spectrum—and researchers realized why every element emits its own distinctive spectrum.

had observed that certain spectra were associated with the atoms of certain elements, but they had never been able to explain why.

Some had found some fascinating mathematical regularities, however. In 1885, Johann Balmer, a mathematical physicist from Switzerland, had found a formula for calculating the wavelengths of the spectral lines of hydrogen. Five years later Johannes Rydberg, a Swedish spectroscopist (a specialist in producing and studying spectral lines), came up with a general formula that could be used to calculate several different line spectra. But these mathematical harmonies served only to deepen the mystery; they offered no explanation.

With his model of the atom, Bohr set out to explain why. He realized that the radius of an electron's orbit was determined by Planck's constant. That meant that the amount of energy also was fixed. An electron in a permissible orbit did not emit any radiation; normally it occupied a stable, basic orbit that Bohr called a ground state.

But if energy was added to the atom, if it was heated, for example, the electron would respond by jumping from one orbit to another—and when it did that, it changed energy states. In response to heat, it would jump to a higher orbit, one farther from the nucleus. If the heat was turned higher, the electron would keep jumping to higher and higher orbits. If it was cooled off, the electron would jump inward to a lower orbit, closer to the nucleus. Moving to a larger orbit, it would absorb energy; moving to a smaller one, it would emit energy. When energy no longer was added, the electron would return to its ground state.

Bohr did the calculations for hydrogen's single electron. He worked out the energies involved for jumping from one orbit that was permissible to another. He calculated the light wavelengths that would be produced if the energy was converted to light. It worked! His calculations matched the spectrum of hydrogen, which always before had been a mystery.

This is what he came up with: Each electron emits a photon (a quantum of light) of characteristic energy, or frequency. The jumps—and the photon energies—are limited by Planck's constant. If the lower-energy state (when the atom is cool and the electron is close to the nucleus) is called W^1, and the higher-energy state is called W^2, you can subtract W^2 from W^1 and the result is hv

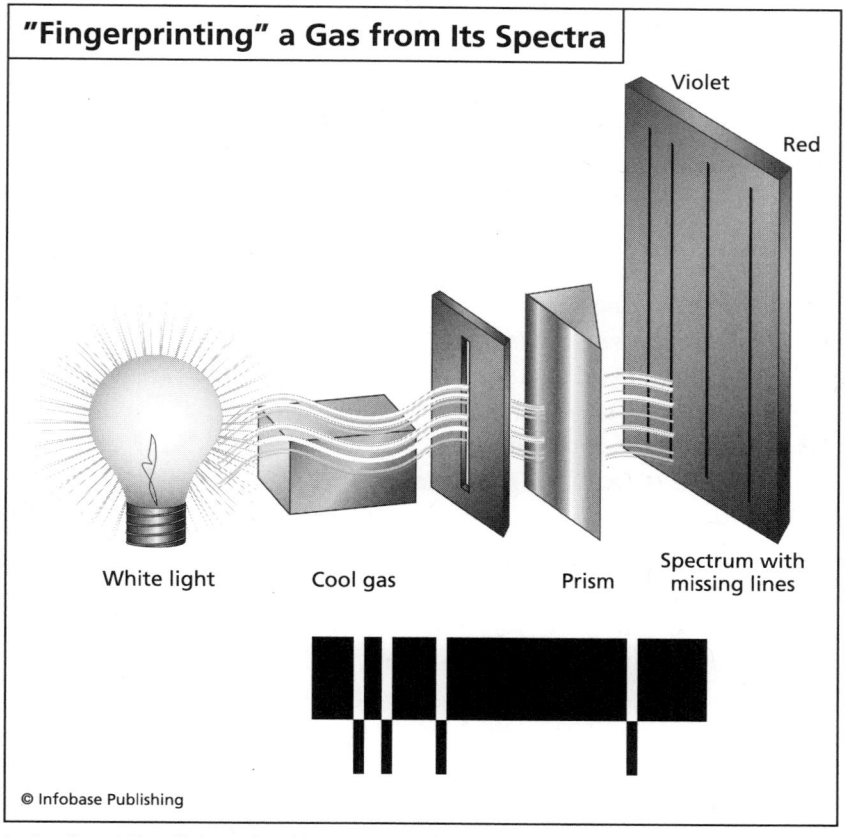

In the illustration, light emitted by an incandescent bulb produces an absorption spectrum when it passes through a sample of cool gas before striking a screen. The gas has absorbed energy from the white light of the bulb, as indicated by the dark lines on the screen. From the pattern of dark lines, it is possible to tell which frequencies the gas has absorbed. Because every element has a unique spectrum, the gas can be identified from the pattern. When an element is heated, it gives off (emits) energy that can be displayed in the same way, producing a similar emission spectrum—a negative, or inversion, of the absorption spectrum. The bottom figure shows the emission and absorption spectra of hydrogen.

(Planck's constant, h, times the frequency, ν). Bohr saw this and, using the formula $W^2 - W^1 = h\nu$, he was able to come up with Balmer's series. He also found that with a slightly more complex formula, using nonarbitrary numbers, representing the mass of the electron, its charge, and Planck's constant, he could come up with Rydberg's experimental values!

Fate of a Paper: ". . . Atoms and Molecules"

As always, Bohr had great difficulty bringing his paper to conclusion. It was getting too long for publication in any journal. Finally he decided to divide it up into three parts. (For this reason, it usually is referred to as the trilogy.) After Bohr had finally finished Part I, "On the Constitution of Atoms and Molecules," he anxiously sent it off to Rutherford on March 6, 1913, and held his breath. In the meantime, he continued to write and rewrite the other two parts.

When Rutherford's letter, dated March 20, finally arrived, Bohr tore it open and scanned it quickly. With the first sentence, he breathed a great sigh of relief.

"I have received your paper safely and read it with great interest," wrote Rutherford, "but I want to look over it again carefully when I have more leisure. Your ideas as to the mode of origin of the spectrum of hydrogen are very ingenious and seem to work out well." But Rutherford's role was to critique and so he did: ". . . but the mixture of Planck's ideas with the old mechanics make it very difficult to form a physical idea of what is the basis of it." And a bit later, he raised a thorny question in a characteristically direct way:

> *There appears to me one grave difficulty in your hypothesis, which I have no doubt you fully realize, namely, how does an electron decide what frequency it is going to vibrate at when it passes from one stationary state to the other? It seems to me that you would have to assume that the electron knows beforehand where it is going to stop.*

Overall, though, Rutherford thought the paper should go off to the *Philosophical Magazine.* He offered to clean up the English for Bohr, and, since he thought it was much too long and wordy, he concluded somewhat casually with the comment, "I suppose you have no objection to my using my judgment to cut out any matter I may consider unnecessary in your paper? Please reply."

Bohr didn't know what to say in reply. He had labored over every sentence, every word of the paper, and was certain that nothing could be cut out without damaging the meaning drastically. But how could he convey a "hands-off" message to Rutherford tactfully? Finally he wrote back that he would be "glad for any alterations you consider suitable," apologizing for any trouble he might have caused, and then concluded offhandedly, "I now have some holidays and I have decided to come over to Manchester." It was a totally unplanned trip, in fact, but it was the only way Bohr could see out of his dilemma.

When Bohr reached Manchester, he was greeted warmly and the two sat right down to work, Rutherford with the idea that at least one-third of the manuscript could be jettisoned. Bohr tenaciously defended the existence of every sentence. Section by section they went through the paper. Section by section Rutherford was won over. In the end, he made only a few corrections to Bohr's English and sent the paper off intact. Later, he loved to tell the story of Bohr's bulldog defense of his words and how he had finally had to give in to the gentle if tenacious Dane.

The second part in Bohr's 1913 trilogy bore the title "Systems Containing Only a Single Nucleus," and the third, "Systems Containing Several Nuclei." All three parts were published by the end of 1913, and Bohr's trilogy became seminally important to physics. It not only offered a highly useful model of the atom, but it showed that quantum mechanics was a fundamental part of how nature worked. While the mechanistic physics of Newton had worked well on larger scales, it could not account for subtleties on the atomic scale. For this work, Bohr would win the 1922 Nobel Prize in physics.

A Look at Bohr's Model

Bohr knew that his model was only a very sketchy approximation of reality, however. Otto Frisch would later recall, "Bohr himself was very much aware of the crudeness of that model; it resembled the atom no more than a quick pencil sketch resembles a living human face. But he also knew how profoundly difficult it would be to get a better picture."

Late in his life Bohr would reflect, "It was clear, and that was *the* point about the Rutherford atom, that we had something from which we could not proceed at all in any other way than by radical change. And that was the reason then that [I] took it up so seriously."

It was radical. It is the threshold of what became known as the heroic age of quantum physics. And the reaction was enormous. Frisch would later recall, "That picture was so astonishing and

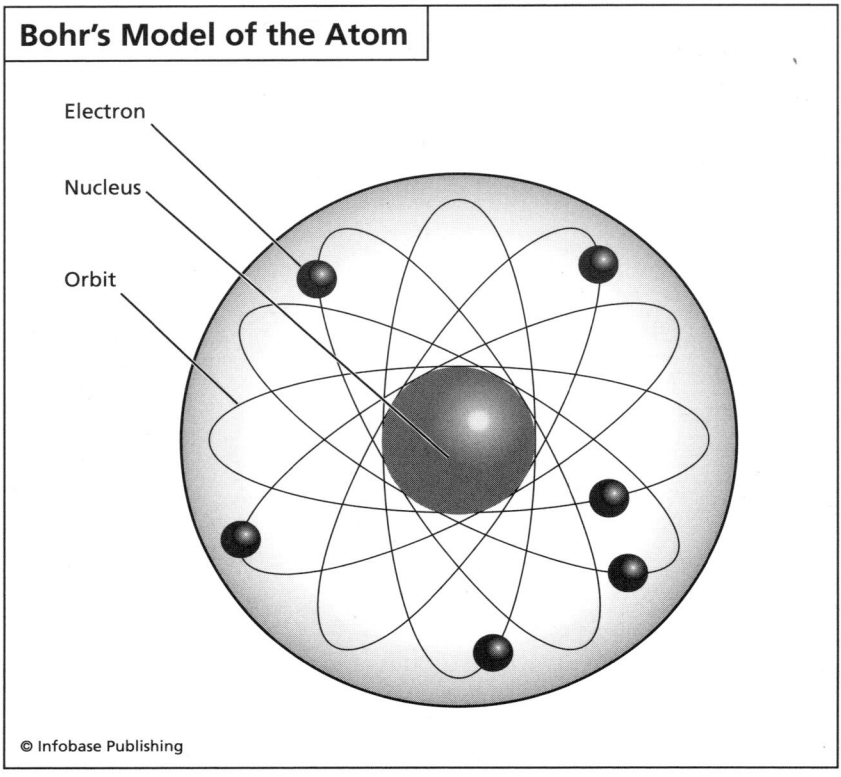

In 1913, Niels Bohr proposed a model of the atom with electrons confined to specific circular orbits around the nucleus.

unorthodox at the time that a number of physicists . . . had sworn to give up physics if that nonsense was true (none of them did)."

Rutherford himself continued to be cautious. In March 1914 he said, "While it is too early to say whether the theories of Bohr are valid, his contributions . . . are of great importance and interest." And in August, "N. Bohr has faced the difficulties by bringing in the idea of the quantum. At all events there is something going on which is inexplicable by the older mechanics."

The old guard was unlikely to be ecstatic. Lord Rayleigh, past 70 by that time, was uninterested. J. J. Thomson did not even comment on Bohr's 1913 papers until 1936.

Even Einstein, a young radical himself, was lukewarm at first. Hevesy told him the news in September 1913 in Vienna, to which

Einstein replied that Bohr's work seemed very interesting and important if right—a polite way of expressing skepticism. Then Hevesy told him about the spectral lines, and Einstein brightened. "This is an enormous achievement," he said. "The theory of Bohr must then be right."

Many years later, when Einstein was almost 70, he wrote:

> *That this insecure and contradictory foundation [of physics in the years from 1910 to 1920] was sufficient to enable a man of Bohr's unique instinct and tact to discover the major laws of the spectral lines and of the electron shells of the atoms together with their significance for chemistry appeared to me like a miracle—and appears to me as a miracle even today. This is the highest form of musicality in the sphere of thought.*

Einstein and Bohr would not meet for another seven years, but during the years that followed publication of Bohr's 1913 trilogy, Einstein kept track of Bohr's work through his writings. He also gathered news from a young physicist named Paul Ehrenfest, of Amsterdam, who struck up a friendship with Bohr by letter in 1918. In a postcard to Max Planck in 1919, Einstein wrote, "Ehrenfest tells me many details from Niels Bohr's *Gedankenküche* [thought kitchen]; his must be a first-rate mind, extremely critical and far-seeing, which never loses track of the grand design."

Harald wrote from Göttingen that people were reading Niels's work with interest, but many seemed to think his premises were too fantastic and too bold. Meanwhile, Bohr spoke at a meeting in Birmingham, England, on September 12, 1913, the first time he presented his work at an international meeting. The write-up in the journal *Nature* said, "Dr. Bohr . . . arrived at a convincing and brilliant explanation of the laws of spectral series."

By the winter of 1914, the University of Copenhagen, impressed by now, invited him to submit his application for appointment as professor of theoretical physics. It would be the first time that theoretical physics was taught at Copenhagen as a separate science, and it was exactly what he wanted. Bohr submitted his application March 4 and wrote to Rutherford, asking for a recommendation, which Rutherford sent back, filled with praise, by return mail. Approval by the faculty was almost unanimous.

But, before the appointment was actually in place, Bohr received another letter from Rutherford that changed everything. An appointment of a two-year readership was available in Manchester, with a stipend of 200 pounds. Rutherford wrote, "I should like to get a young fellow with some originality in him." Namely, Bohr.

Back to Manchester

Premonitions of war were brewing in Germany at this time, but for the most part, people thought war was unlikely, and Bohr couldn't pass up an opportunity to work directly with Rutherford. He quickly arranged with the University of Copenhagen to wait two years for him and made preparations to head back to Manchester.

On June 28, 1914, the Archduke Francis Ferdinand of Austria-Hungary was assassinated by a Serb extremist. Austria-Hungary issued an ultimatum to the Serbian government, and Germany promised support. Tensions that had been seething for years suddenly sent the world to the brink of war. Russia mobilized against Austria, and on August 1, Germany declared war on Russia. Denmark, as always, was vulnerable. German and British fleets prowled the waters, and one sea battle took place on August 28. Travel to Manchester now looked risky.

But by September, although war in Europe continued, travel between Denmark and England by sea again seemed safe, and the Bohrs set out for Manchester. There Bohr produced another paper for the *Philosophical Magazine* in 1915, "On the Quantum Theory of Radiation and the Structure of the Atom," strengthening the points of his previous work. As before, the work in Manchester was exhilarating, intense, and always productive. To Bohr, it was an object lesson in how he might run his own department of theoretical physics in Copenhagen, when he returned.

By 1916, as Bohr was preparing his notes and papers to return to Denmark, the war had grown grimmer. Rutherford sent a letter with Bohr to protect his notes from confiscation, certifying that they were intended for English scientific publication. Although the guns in Europe roared on, the Bohrs returned safely home.

Papers by other scientists were beginning to come out that were offshoots of Bohr's theory, and he was having to work hard to keep ahead. Three years had passed since his famous trilogy had been published, and confirming experimental results were beginning to pile up. So were the offers. Before the year was out, Bohr had received an invitation from the University of California to spend a year there. Soon after, the University of Manchester invited him to join its faculty. But the war made California an unlikely destination, and Bohr asked Manchester to wait a few months for his decision. Meanwhile, in November 1916, the Bohrs had their first son, Christian, an event they both rejoiced in greatly. Five other children, all boys, would follow in the years to come: Hans Henrik (born in 1918), Erik (1920), Aage Niels (1922), Ernest David (1924, named after both their good friend Rutherford and Niels's maternal grandfather), and Harald (1928). Bohr loved his children and always managed to spend time with them, despite his fast-paced schedule.

Throughout 1916, Bohr continued to work on publications, finding them difficult to complete, as always, and he continued an active correspondence with Rutherford, the news of whose research he followed with great interest. But now his attention was also greatly drawn to his teaching. At first his classes in theoretical physics drew only a handful of advanced students, primarily those interested in quantum theory. (Knudsen, the only other physics professor at the university, had no use for quantum theory. One student who took classes from both of them recalled Knudsen's sharp response to a question involving it: "If we have to use quantum theory to explain this, we may as well not explain it.") Gradually, as Bohr delved more and more into atomic theory in his classes, faculty members began turning up too. The discussions went deep and Bohr pushed his students' thinking, chalk in hand, furrowed brow, expectant smile, waiting for the next thought. His was a kindly, responsive face. Abraham Pais, a physicist from Holland who later became his biographer, once wrote of his first meeting with Bohr, "My first thought was, what a gloomy face." But this first impression melted immediately. Those who knew Bohr were captured by the sunny, warm smile and the animation that came to his face when he talked.

By 1917 Bohr had approached the university about an idea he had—the establishment of a small institute for theoretical physics as part of the university. Soon after the war's end, the plan was approved. Bohr was able to raise about $20,000 toward the construction of a building, and Copenhagen made a site available adjacent to a park near the center of the city. In his enthusiasm, Bohr immediately invited the Rutherfords to the inauguration, which was still several years off.

Ripple Effect and Two Offers

All these plans nearly toppled, however, when a letter arrived from Rutherford. It had been delayed by the disruption of the mails caused by the confusion as the war ended. It was marked "private and confidential." Rutherford was offering Bohr a permanent position as professor of mathematical physics at a new center for modern physics research at Manchester. He wrote:

> *You know how delighted we would be to see you working with us again. I think the two of us could try and make physics boom. Well think it over and let me know your mind as soon as you can. Possibly you might think of visiting us as soon as the seas are clear.*

Rutherford concluded his letter, "I wish I had you here to discuss the meaning of some of my results on collisions of nuclei. I think I have got some rather startling results."

This last was Rutherford's strongest card. What a team they might make! It was an opportunity without parallel—wonderful and impossible at the same time. Niels and Margrethe hurried to discuss the new turn of events with Harald. They talked all day and into the night. In the end, though, there was no question. Bohr was a Dane, and he could not turn his back on Denmark, when the country had offered him everything he had asked for. He had to stay and build his own center for modern physics research, in Copenhagen. Bohr felt, at that moment, that he might not be making the best decision either for his scientific work or his family's financial welfare. Working with Rutherford, he might accomplish insights he might never have on his own, and Denmark could not offer him the salary that the English university could. But he made the only ethical decision he could make. Rutherford did not give up immediately, but in the end, Bohr stayed to build an institute for Denmark.

And build he did, from the ground up. Every detail of the architect's drawings had to meet with his approval. He went to the site every day to oversee the progress during construction, and he watch-dogged at every turn. He may have driven the architect and construction crews crazy, and he certainly slowed the progress, but in the end the institute was built exactly to his specifications.

Already by the 1920s, when this photo was taken, Bohr had become well known and respected for his ability and intensity. (Niels Bohr Archive, Copenhagen)

Rutherford, meanwhile, was offered the directorship of the Cavendish Laboratory at Cambridge, which he accepted. Bohr took time off in July 1919 to visit him and consult with him about his work. He also lectured in Holland, where he and other physicists talked about atomic problems nonstop. Arnold Sommerfeld, the first of the German scientists to venture into the previously neutral countries, went to Copenhagen, where he and Bohr talked about quantum theory and atomic structure.

For a time the institute ran out of construction funds, as costs raced sky-high in the postwar economy. Always resourceful, Bohr obtained a grant from the Carlsberg Beer Company in Copenhagen, and construction resumed.

Enter Einstein

Despite his busy schedule, when Max Planck invited him to go to Berlin to lecture on spectral theory at the *Physikalische Gesellschaft* (Physics Society), Bohr quickly agreed, and it was a decision he never regretted. There, as he arrived at the Berlin physics building, Planck and Albert Einstein came out to greet him. Planck looked formal and proper, as he smiled warmly behind wire-rimmed glasses. Einstein, with his wild halo of hair, never looked formal, on that day or any other day. The three men began discussing atomic physics immediately and continued, morning to night, for the rest of the conference, whenever they weren't in meetings.

Einstein had formulated the general statistical rules for the electron jumps from one of Bohr's stationary states to another. These jumps could occur, he said, not just in response to radiation or collision. They could occur spontaneously.

Bohr, meanwhile, suggested in his lecture on spectral theory that an exact determination of where and when electrons jump could not be made. This Einstein did not like. No theory should leave to chance the time and determination of fundamental processes, he maintained. Here, already, the two great minds began to take divergent paths. Their conversations revolved around these themes and left a deep impression on Bohr, as he continued to mull them over in his thoughts.

"With his mastery for coordinating apparently contrasting experience," Bohr later wrote, "without abandoning continuity and causality, Einstein was perhaps more reluctant to renounce such ideals than someone for whom renunciation . . . appeared to be the only way to proceed with the immediate task of coordinating the multifarious evidence regarding atomic phenomena."

Two days after the end of the conference, Einstein wrote to Ehrenfest, "Bohr was here, and I am as much in love with him as you are. He is like an extremely sensitive child who moves around in this world in a sort of trance."

And to Einstein, Bohr wrote, "To meet you and talk with you was one of the greatest experiences I ever had."

In September 1921, the inauguration of the Institute for Theoretical Physics in Copenhagen took place, and Bohr became its head at the age of 36. From the time the institute was built, the Bohrs lived in a flat on the upper level of the research center's only building. In 1924, Bohr bought a summer home as a retreat in Tisvilde on the island of Sjaelland (where Copenhagen is located), 40 miles northwest of the Danish capital, near the shore of the Kattegat strait, which lies between Denmark and Sweden. An old gamekeeper's home, the house was a one-story cottage with a thatched roof. Its name was *Lynghuset,* meaning "heather house," and it was nestled among rolling hills dotted with heather shrubs

The Institute for Theoretical Physics in Copenhagen was a single, lonely building waiting for students at the time of its inauguration in 1921. (Niels Bohr Archive, Copenhagen)

and high pine forests. A small one-room cabin, which they called *Pavillonen* (the pavilion), stood nearby the house—the perfect place for Bohr and his colleagues to work undisturbed. The peaceful surroundings of Tisvilde provided the Bohrs with the ideal summer retreat, a much-needed place to get away from the pressures of their intense daily life.

But from the start Bohr's life revolved around the new institute. There, like a magnet, Bohr drew the best young minds from all over the world. Georg von Hevesy, from his days at Manchester, was one of the first of many foreigners Bohr invited to come to Denmark to work in the new institute. Fueled with the exciting discoveries of radioactivity, quantum theory, and relativity, in its first 25 or 30 years the 20th century witnessed an enormous outpouring of ideas and discoveries unparalleled in the history of physics. A dynamic cluster of men and women—ambitious, brilliant, keenly prepared, and talented—gathered in the universities of Europe, Britain, and, to a lesser degree, Canada and the United States to ride the crest of a great wave of exploration into the inner regions of the atom. Niels Bohr's institute rapidly became a point of reference for all these young physicists, led by the man who came to be known as the "Gentle Dane."

Niels's easygoing sense of humor and charismatic way of drawing ideas out of people stimulated endless discussion. As Otto Frisch, who was a young student at the institute, described him:

> *He had a soft voice with a Danish accent, and we were not always sure whether he was speaking English or German; he spoke both with equal ease and kept switching. Here, I felt, was Socrates come to life, tossing us challenges in his gentle way, lifting each argument to a higher plane, drawing wisdom out of us which we didn't know we had, and which of course we hadn't.*

As a teacher and mentor, he was unrivaled.

4

Bohr and Einstein: Battle between Friends

(1925–1929)

During the 1920s and 1930s, the Institute for Theoretical Physics in Copenhagen, headed by Bohr, commanded an influence over the world of scientific thought equaled only by Aristotle's Lyceum in Athens. Theoretical physicists went there from all over the world, during a time often called the heroic age of atomic physics. These were the same years—especially 1925 to 1927—that in Göttingen are known as the years of *Knabenphysik*, "boyhood physics." Breakthrough after breakthrough was made by very young scientists: Werner Heisenberg, at 23; Wolfgang Pauli, at 25; Paul Dirac, at 22. At 37, Erwin Schrödinger, by contrast, seemed out of place. All of these found their way to Niels Bohr's institute and felt the influence of Bohr the mentor, himself only in his early 40s. One by one, each carved out a place for himself in the quantum physics hall of fame. The year 1925, in particular, was a great year in physics, especially quantum physics.

Pauli's Exclusion Principle

Wolfgang Pauli was clumsy in the lab and faltering in front of a lecture hall full of listeners. Yet his mind could pierce to the heart of a problem seemingly without effort. He studied under Arnold Sommerfeld at the University of Munich, where he did his doctoral work, and then pursued postgraduate studies both in Copenhagen with Bohr and at Göttingen. (Later he moved to the United States,

An Unlikely Friendship: Wolfgang Pauli and Carl Jung

Of all the young and brilliant men who orbited Niels Bohr, Wolfgang Pauli was one of the more enigmatic and colorful. Quite aware of his own brilliance, he published a 200-page article on relativity for *The Encyclopedia of Mathematical Sciences* when he was only 21 years old. Einstein himself was greatly impressed, writing in 1922:

> *Who ever studies this mature and grandly composed work would not believe that the author is a man of twenty-one. One does not know what to admire most: the psychological understanding of the evolution of ideas, the accuracy of mathematical deduction, the deep physical insight, the capacity for lucid systematic presentation, the knowledge of literature, the factual completeness, or the infallibility of criticism.*

It was heady praise on which to start a career.

Demanding much of himself, Pauli also demanded much from his scientific colleagues. His scathing criticisms—"I don't mind you thinking slowly, but I mind your publishing much faster than you think"—are still quoted today. Many of his letters were signed "The scourge of God," and he could often be seen, as he listened to papers being presented by his colleagues, leaning forward in his chair, his oversized head bobbing up and down as he analyzed each line of reasoning.

joining the Institute for Advanced Study in Princeton, and becoming a citizen in 1946.)

His great insight, known as Pauli's exclusion principle, came to him as he was battling a problem known as the anomalous Zeeman effect. Moody and dejected while visiting Bohr, he replied snappishly to Margrethe Bohr's solicitous inquiry, "Of course I am unhappy! I cannot understand the anomalous Zeeman effect."

Pauli based his work on an enormous pile of data, in which he discerned a simple sorting-out principle that held true in all cases: In any system of elementary particles—for example, the collection of electrons within the atom—no two particles may move in the

Still, though caustic, his criticisms were eagerly sought, and getting Pauli's approval automatically made someone's day.

Brilliance, though, does not guarantee an easy life, and for much of his life Pauli fought deep depression that began in his early thirties when his much-loved mother committed suicide in 1927 and his first marriage to a nightclub singer ended in a bitter divorce in 1930. Close to a nervous breakdown and following his father's advice, he sought the help of the psychoanalyst Carl Jung, being analyzed first by one of Jung's assistants and then by Jung himself. It was the beginning of a surprising relationship between the two men that lasted for many years and included the publication of a volume of joint essays. Erudite and well read, Pauli had always managed to keep philosophy out of his physics but had long sought some deeper understanding of life. Jungian analysis and its quasi-scientific approach to opening doors of perception obviously struck a chord with Pauli and, under Jung's instructions, he even kept a careful record of more than 1,000 of his dreams.

While it appeared disquieting to many that Pauli, the razor-sharp rationalist, should become a part of Jung's mystical worldview, the relationship obviously meant much to Pauli. As Pauli lay dying, Jung was the only person Pauli wanted to see on his deathbed.

same way, that is, occupy the same energy state. He announced this "Exclusion Principle" in 1925.

The Exclusion Principle explained why electrons in an atom do not all drop down to the orbit nearest the nucleus—which might normally be expected, since an electron traveling along the smallest, closest ring requires the least amount of energy to complete an orbit. According to Pauli's principle, once an electron is in an orbit, it excludes any other electron from occupying the same orbit. Over the years Pauli's Exclusion Principle has proved to hold true for nuclear particles that no one had even dreamed of, and it has been a key concept in the development of quantum mechanics. Pauli received the Nobel Prize in physics (somewhat belatedly) for this work in 1945.

Wave-Particle Duality

In Paris, meanwhile, Louis de Broglie proposed an idea, known as the wave-particle duality, that ended up bothering Albert Einstein a great deal. De Broglie maintained that if atomic particles were also thought of as waves, not just particles, the consequences theoretically were very nice, even though the idea is mind-boggling.

Erwin Schrödinger is best known today for a paradox he called "Schrödinger's Cat." (Francis Simon, courtesy AIP Emilio Segrè Visual Archives)

According to Planck and Einstein, light, which had most recently been regarded as a wave, should be regarded as a particle. Now de Broglie was saying that particles—photons, electrons, even atoms—sometimes behave like waves. Outlandish as this sounds, experimental tests bear out de Broglie's theory.

The idea immediately caught on among many physicists. In 1926, Erwin Schrödinger came up with an equation that accurately described the way an electron behaves. Schrödinger interpreted his equation, known as "wave mechanics," to represent that electrons *are* de Broglie's waves. Swept up in the wave concept, Schrödinger wanted to abandon completely the idea that electrons are particles.

But on this point Schrödinger was wrong. Schrödinger's theory of wave mechanics worked beautifully, and physicists loved it for its perfect accuracy, but in June of the same year, Max Born published a paper that instead gave electron waves a probabilistic interpretation.

Born said the rise and fall of waves could be taken to indicate the rise and fall in *probability* that the electron behaved as a particle.

In this brief, basic paper, Born went straight to the crux of the problem of cause and effect. In the macroworld of classical mechanics, cause and effect might work as a principle, but not in the subtle microworld where quantum mechanics ruled. Regarding atomic collisions, Born wrote:

> *One does not get an answer to the question, What is the state after collision? but only to the question, How probable is a given effect of the collision?... From the standpoint of our quantum mechanics, there is no quantity which causally fixes the effect of a collision in an individual event. Should we hope to discover such properties later ... and determine [them] in individual events?... I myself am inclined to renounce determinism in the atomic world, but that is a philosophical question for which physical arguments alone do not set standards.*

Basically, Born had abandoned causality in the classical sense. Leon Lederman, one of the world's top physicists in the 1990s, calls Max Born's interpretation "the single most dramatic and major change in our world view since Newton." Yet Schrödinger was not happy with Born's idea at all, and neither were many other classical physicists of his day. Born's probability meant that the determinism promised by Newton's laws of physics could no longer be relied upon. Coupled with quantum theory, it meant that only probabilities could be known—about anything you wanted to measure.

By 1926–27, Albert Einstein, who already had a towering reputation in physics, began to reject many of the bizarre implications of quantum mechanics. Replying to one of Born's letters, Einstein wrote: "Quantum mechanics is very impressive. But an inner voice tells me that it is not yet the real thing. The theory produces a good deal but hardly brings us closer to the secret of the Old One. I am at all events convinced that *He* does not play dice."

In February 1927, Einstein gave a lecture in Berlin, in which he reportedly said, "What nature demands from us is not a quantum theory or a wave theory; rather, nature demands from us a synthesis of these two views which thus far has exceeded the mental powers of physicists."

But Bohr, Sommerfeld, Heisenberg, and others took Born's ideas in stride—the concepts seemed logical—and they and their colleagues continued the exciting work of trying to get all the pieces to fit. It was great teamwork. It was also the beginning of a friendly but impassioned lifelong debate between Bohr and Einstein, which would continue for more than a quarter of a century until Einstein's death in 1955.

Heisenberg: Uncertainty and Quantum Theory

The issues heated up in March 1927, when Werner Heisenberg produced another amazing physical theory: the Uncertainty Principle. According to that principle, the exact position and precise velocity of an electron could not be determined at the same time. In other words, no one can tell for certain where an electron will go when it is hit—all that can be said is where it probably will go. Only statistical predictions can be made.

This idea capped off the great scientific revolution we call quantum theory. (Although much remained to be wrapped up and quantum field theory is still evolving today. Some scientists contend that the theory will not be complete until it is fully combined with gravitation, and many have attempted to formulate a unified field theory that would accomplish this goal.) The work of Born, Schrödinger and Heisenberg formed the basis for quantum mechanics, which has been used to interpret chemistry and subatomic physics with great success. Yet Einstein never accepted the Uncertainty Principle, and he debated long and ardently with Bohr about it.

In September 1927 Bohr attended a meeting in Colma, Italy. (Einstein had been invited, but he did not attend.) There, on

September 16, Bohr outlined for the first time the principle he called "complementarity":

> *The very nature of the quantum theory . . . forces us to regard the space-time coordination and the claim of causality, the union of which characterizes the classical theories, as complementary but exclusive features of the description, symbolizing the idealization of observation and definition, respectively.*

Bohr maintained that a phenomenon can be looked upon in two mutually exclusive ways, and yet both outlooks can remain valid in their own terms. For example, you may know the momentum or the position of an electron, but not both. As his student Frisch put it, "It is a bit as if reality was painted on both sides of a canvas so that you could only see one aspect of it clearly at any time." Complementarity would become the cornerstone of Bohr's thinking about quantum and classical physics, his way of reconciling two equally plausible but mutually exclusive ideas.

Albert Einstein and Niels Bohr talked fervently whenever they could find the time, exploring the complexities of atomic physics together, such as this opportunity, probably at the Solvay Conference of 1930. (Paul Ehrenfast, courtesy AIP Emilio Segrè Visual Archives, Ehrenfast Collection)

Brilliant, vital, and exciting ideas, the emerging concepts of quantum physics were also unsettling. Even Bohr, having put quantum to its first use in the physics of matter, recognized the theory's enormous mysteries.

"It makes me quite giddy to think about these problems," a visitor once complained to Bohr. "But, but,

The Clock in a Box

At the fifth Solvay Conference in October 1927, all the founders of the quantum theory were present: Max Planck, Albert Einstein (a founder in spite of himself), Niels Bohr, Louis de Broglie, Werner Heisenberg, Erwin Schrödinger, Wolfgang Pauli, and Paul Dirac.

At session after session, Einstein sat silent. At one point he voiced a simple objection to the probability interpretation. Then he fell back into silence. He had declined an invitation to give a paper on quantum statistics at the conference.

But not all the important discussions took place on the floor of the meetings. As described by Otto Stern, the informal discussions in cafés and breakfast rooms tended to exude far more vitality:

> *Einstein came down to breakfast and expressed his misgivings about the new quantum theory, every time [he] had invented some beautiful experiment from which one saw that [the theory] did not work . . . Pauli and Heisenberg, who were there, did not pay much attention, "ach was, das stimmt schon, das stimmt schon" [ah, well, it will be all right, it will be all right]. Bohr, on the other hand, reflected on it with care and in the evening, at dinner, we were all together and he cleared up the matter in detail.*

The debate continued at the next Solvay Conference (on magnetism), held in 1930. Einstein came prepared. He had been thinking, and he believed he had come up with an example that disproved the validity of the uncertainty principle. Imagine, he said, that you have a box. A hole in one of the walls of the box can be opened and closed by a shutter, which is controlled by a clock inside the box. You fill the box with radiation and weigh the box. Set the shutter to open just long enough for a single photon to escape. Afterward, weigh the box again. At this point, Einstein maintained, the experimenter has succeeded in finding both the photon energy and its time of passage—which is exactly what Heisenberg's uncertainty principle says cannot be done.

Bohr was stumped—shocked, in fact. With his clock-in-a-box thought experiment, Einstein had apparently found a way around the dilemma of uncertainty that Heisenberg had posed. As one observer later wrote:

> *During the whole evening [Bohr] was extremely unhappy, going from one to the other and trying to persuade them that it couldn't be true, that it would be the end of physics if Einstein*

Bohr's View of Einstein's Clock-in-a-Box Experiment

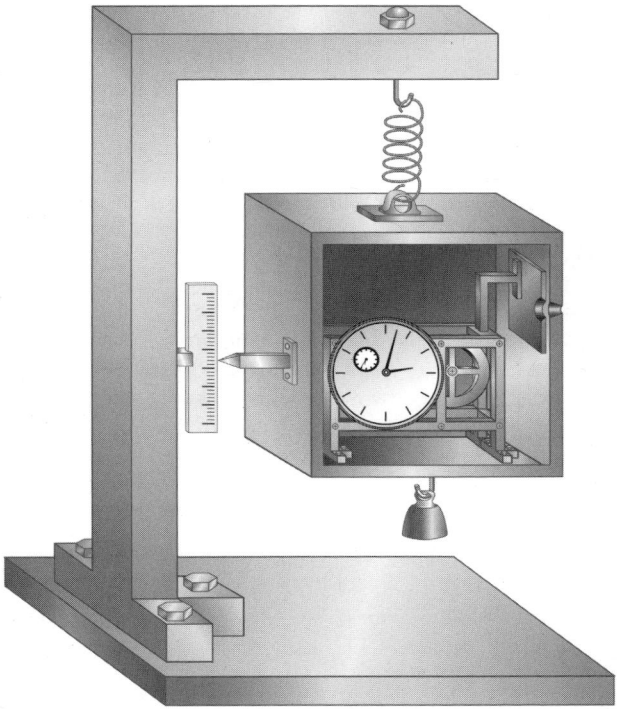

© Infobase Publishing

One of Bohr and Einstein's most puzzling thought experiments was the clock-in-a-box.

> *were right, but he couldn't produce any refutation. I shall never forget the vision of the two antagonists leaving . . . : Einstein a tall majestic figure, walking quietly, with a somewhat ironical smile, and Bohr trotting near him, very excited.*

(continues on next page)

(continued from previous page)

By the next morning, however, the tables were turned. Bohr had an answer. He had realized a point that Einstein, ironically, had forgotten: that one of the subtle effects of Einstein's general theory of relativity was the production of the very time uncertainty the thought experiment was supposed to disprove. Bohr used Einstein's same idea of a clock in a box, but he added realistic experimental details that Einstein had not bothered with. Later he used a diagram to illustrate the point. The initial weighing is done by recording the position of a pointer attached to the box suspended from the scale, which is attached to a fixed frame. The weight measurement is uncertain (with the pointer returning to its initial position when the photon escapes). And the uncertainty of the position of the clock in the gravitational field also implies another uncertainty in the determination of time.

Bohr had showed that if you actually performed the experiment, with real equipment, the accuracy with which the energy of the photon is measured would restrict the precision with which its moment of escape can be determined. Einstein's thought experiment did not violate the uncertainty relations for energy and time, after all. Bohr provided details on all the facets of the apparatus that would be required to take the measurements in a classical physics setting. Heavy bolts hold the frame steady. The spring keeps the box mobile in the gravitational field. The weight of the box readjusts the position.

but . . ." Bohr stammered ingenuously, "if anybody says he can think about quantum theory without getting giddy it merely shows that he hasn't understood the first thing about it!"

As the brilliant American theoretical physicist Richard Feynman used to say to his students, "I think it is safe to say that no one understands quantum mechanics. Do not keep saying to yourself, if you possibly can avoid it, 'But how can it be like that?' because you will go 'down the drain,' into a blind alley from which nobody has yet escaped. Nobody knows how it can be like that."

During the years from 1925 to 1929 Bohr gave many lectures on this complex topic, and his listeners valiantly strove to follow along. But not everyone was successful at keeping up. As Richard Courant recounted, at one point during the "grand period of the evolving quantum theory" Bohr was laid up from a skiing accident, with only Harald and Courant to listen to him. Bohr began trying to explain to them the "just-evolving ideas about basic principles of quantum physics and complementarity." But when the two nonphysicists got lost, they interrupted for an explanation of some incomprehensible points. "It was a typical Bohr lecture such as we all have experienced so often," Courant said, "excitingly inspiring, though neither acoustically nor otherwise completely understandable." When interrupted, though, Bohr protested angrily: "Of course you cannot understand what I try to say now; this may perhaps become understandable, but only after you have heard the story as a whole and have understood the end."

Bohr's ability to think literally had served him once again. Sometimes his literal-mindedness crept into strange contexts, however. One of Bohr's young colleagues from those days recollected times when he and his friends would talk Bohr into an evening at the movies:

> *We had great preference for bad films. Sometimes we could entice Bohr to come with us to see a Western or a gangster film we had selected. His comments were always remarkable because he used to introduce some of his ideas on observations and measurements. Once, after a thoroughly stupid Tom Mix film, his verdict went about as follows: "I did not like that picture; it was too improbable. That the scoundrel runs off with the beautiful girl is logical; it always happens. That the bridge collapses under their carriage is unlikely, but I am willing to accept it. That the heroine remains suspended in mid-air over a precipice is even more unlikely, but again I accept it. I am even willing to accept that at that very moment Tom Mix is coming by on his horse. But that at that very moment there should be a fellow with a motion picture camera to film the whole business—that is more than I am willing to believe."*

These were years of great discovery. Naturally, debate ensued. It is the job of science to question, and Einstein and others who questioned were doing their jobs as scientists, just as those who set forth hypotheses were doing their jobs. As the physicist Robert Oppenheimer would later write of this period in physics:

Our understanding of atomic physics, of what we call the quantum theory of atomic systems, had its origins at the turn of the century and its great synthesis and resolutions in the nineteen-twenties. It was a heroic time. It was not the doing of any one man. It involved the collaboration of scores of scientists from many different lands, though from first to last the deeply creative and subtle and critical spirit of Niels Bohr guided, restrained, deepened and finally transmuted the enterprise. It was a period of patient work in the laboratory, of crucial experiments and daring action, of many false starts and many untenable conjectures. It was a time of earnest correspondence and hurried conference, of debate, criticism and brilliant mathematical improvisation. For those who participated it was a time of creation. There was terror as well as exaltation in their new insight.

5

The "Spirit of Copenhagen"

(1930–1938)

During the early 1930s, Bohr guided the physicists of his institute into the realm of theoretical nuclear physics. The new era began in August 1928, when George Gamow, a talented young physicist from Odessa, stopped at Copenhagen on his way back to the Soviet Union after his postdoctoral work in Göttingen. As he later told the story, he detoured to Copenhagen to meet Bohr, but had only $10 in his pocket, lodging for only one night, and no food. He urgently told Bohr's secretary that he had to see Bohr that day—he could not afford to stay longer. So Bohr met with Gamow and discussed with him the paper on gamma rays that Gamow had been working on in Germany. Then Bohr said, "My secretary told me you cannot stay more than one day because you have no money. Now if I organize for you a fellowship . . . would you stay for a year?"

"Yes, I would," Gamow replied quickly. And so it was done, on the spot, and Gamow stayed not one but two years, from 1928–29.

During the last month of his stay, Gamow completed his book on radioactivity and atomic nuclei. It was the first book on theoretical nuclear physics ever written. So began an era of nuclear investigation at Bohr's institute.

Exploring Atomic Structure

It was a field full of major activity in the 1930s. The stage had been set by Rutherford, in England, in 1919. Continuing his experiments, he decided to try firing alpha particles through a tube of nitrogen gas. When he examined the results, he discovered something strange. In addition to his alpha-particle bullets (emitted naturally by radioactive radium), he found particles that had the same properties as hydrogen nuclei, even though the tube contained no hydrogen. (These particles later were called protons.) Rutherford concluded that the alpha particles had struck a few nitrogen nuclei and split the hydrogen nuclei away. While the discovery of radioactivity had shown that certain atoms could disintegrate spontaneously in nature,

In 1930, Bohr and his institute held a conference that was well attended, with many of the participants numbering among the most productive scientists in the world. Seated in the front row, left to right: Oskar Klein, Niels Bohr, Werner Heisenberg, Wolfgang Pauli, George Gamow, Lev Landau, and Hendrik Kramers. (Niels Bohr Archive, Copenhagen)

this was the first evidence that ordinary (nonradioactive) atoms were not indestructible. Over the next five years, with his colleague James Chadwick, Rutherford tried similar experiments skimming off protons from the nuclei of 10 different elements with alpha bullets. From these experiments they began to realize that the nucleus was not just a tiny positively charged entity; they were probing it, and if it could be probed, and chunks could be broken off in this way, it must have an internal structure—it must be composed of particles. The question was, what particles?

Perhaps, Rutherford hypothesized, there was a third, neutral, atomic particle not yet discovered. It was a reasonable idea, since protons alone could not account for the atomic weight of any atom except hydrogen. Lithium, for example, has only three protons, and yet its atomic weight is seven. The negative charge of electrons balanced the protons' positive charge. Yet the mass of electrons, the only other known particle, was negligible. Where did all the rest of the weight come from?

Irène and Frédéric Joliot-Curie, in the tradition of Irène's parents, Marie and Pierre Curie, also were actively exploring atomic structure, in Paris. In their experiments they had been bombarding beryllium with alpha particles, and they were getting a strange particle they thought was a type of penetrating radiation, like a gamma ray. Bohr wrote to Rutherford, however, that he didn't think they were right. James Chadwick, who was working with Rutherford, tried a similar series of experiments. He spent day and night at the lab for three weeks straight, finally coming up with proof of the existence of Rutherford's neutral particle.

Rutherford shot the news off to Bohr, who was delighted. In Copenhagen, he and his colleagues confirmed the results. The neutron was discovered, successfully accounting for all the excess weight on the periodic table.

Bohr and the Atomic Nucleus

Bohr now became intrigued by the dynamics of the nucleus, and in April 1932 he gave a lecture on the neutron's properties. He wrote to Heisenberg, drawing him into the quest, and Heisenberg sat down and roughed out a basic proton-neutron model of the nucleus. "The

Bohr took mentoring seriously, challenging his students and colleagues with a soft voice and big questions. In this photo, Bohr (left) meets with James Franck (center) and Hans Marius Hansen. (AIP Emilio Segrè Visual Archives, Margrethe Bohr Collection)

basic idea," he wrote to Bohr in June, "is to shove all difficulties of principle onto the neutron and then apply quantum mechanics to the nucleus." It was a beginning.

During these years, Bohr was at the nexus of communication among colleagues all over the world, and his interpretative advice was greatly respected. He loved a paradox: Out of paradox, he believed, would come progress. And he had a talent for giving focus, meaning, and direction to lines of inquiry. In this way, he influenced the scientific process in nearly every country in the world.

By this time the study of nuclear physics began to demand ways of accelerating the bombarding particles more effectively, and in England John Cockroft and Ernest Thomas Sinton Walton invented the first particle accelerator in 1929. By 1935 Bohr had negotiated for a similar model for the institute at Copenhagen, and design studies began for its construction. Though the laboratory was small, Bohr wanted it to remain on the cutting edge of the field of nuclear physics.

The Physicists' Parody of *Faust*

Despite Bohr's stature and influence—by now he had received dozens of awards, including the Faraday medal, in addition to the Nobel Prize—his rapport with his students and colleagues remained high-spirited and open, as evidenced by the following parody of *Faust,* staged by some of his students for an annual September celebration, sometime in the early 1930s. Wolfgang Pauli played the part of Mephisto, and the Lord, played by another student, is obviously meant to represent Bohr, who was present in the audience:

BOHR (the Lord):
Hast thou naught else to say?
Comest thou ever with complaining?
Is physics never to thy mind?
PAULI (Mephisto):
Nay, 'tis all folly! Rotten, as ever, to the core!
E'en in my days of dule it grieves me sore
and I must ever plague these physicists the more.
B.: (In the mixture of German and English he always used when excited): *Oh, it is dreadful! In this situation we must remember the essential failure of classical concepts . . . muss ich sagen . . . just a little remark . . . what do you propose to do with mass?*
P.: What's that got to do with it? Mass? We must abolish it!
B.: Well, that's very, very interesting . . . but . . . but—
P.: No, shut up! Stop talking rubbish!
B.: But . . . but—
P.: I forbid you to speak!
B.: But Pauli! Pauli! We're really much more in agreement than you think! Of course, I quite agree! Only . . . Certainly, we can abolish mass. But we must uphold load. . . .
P.: What for? Why? No, no, that's wishful thinking! Why not abolish load, too?
B.: I must ask . . . I understand perfectly, of course . . . but . . . but—
P.: Silence!
B.: But Pauli, you must really give me a chance to finish what I have to say! If both mass and load are abolished, what have we got left?

(continues on next page)

(continued from previous page)

P.: Oh, that's quite simple! What we've got left will be the neutron!
(Pause. Both pace to and fro.)
B.: It's not to criticize, it's but to learn.
I take my leave now, later to return.
(Exit.)
P.: (Soliloquizes):
I like to see the old chap now and then and take good care we don't fall out. It's jolly decent of so grand a Lord, I must say, when he comes himself for a nice chat with Pauli!
(Exit.)

Meanwhile, Bohr had been working on a new theory, featuring what he called a compound nucleus. The idea that the nucleus was a single rigid body, he said, was incorrect and misleading. Further, he maintained, nuclear reactions took place in two stages. In the first stage, during bombardment of a nucleus by a projectile, the projectile (of whatever kind—alpha particle, neutron, and so on) merges with the nucleus, forming a compound nucleus. In the second stage, this compound nucleus comes apart—in one of three ways. It may disintegrate into the original particles that made it up, unchanged by the bombardment. Or it may break up into the same particles, but excited (that is, raised to a higher energy level). Or it may form new particles (through nuclear reaction). Bohr's ideas received rapid and wide acceptance in the nuclear physics community and produced considerable impetus for further testing and extension of his model.

In December 1931, Niels Bohr was invited to become a permanent resident at the Residence of Honor on the grounds of the Carlsberg breweries, an honor bestowed for life on the citizen of Denmark considered the most prominent in the sciences or the arts. The vote by the governing committee in this case was unanimous. Niels and Margrethe moved to Carlsberg in the summer of 1932, with their six sons; their first house guests, appropriately, were Ernest and Mary Rutherford, who visited in September of that year.

Intellectual Heights at Bohr's Institute

By 1935 Otto Frisch had arrived in Copenhagen and was deeply impressed by the vibrant man who ran the institute. As Frisch wrote in his memoirs:

> *Niels Bohr was fifty then and at the height of his powers, both mentally and physically. He was heavily built, but when he thundered up the stairs two steps at a time we young ones found it hard to keep up with him. He also beat us all at table tennis.*

In the evenings, the students usually went to Carlsberg for food and talk.

> *After dinner, we would sit around Bohr, some of us on the floor at his feet to watch him first fill his pipe and then to hear what he said. . . . Our conversation ranged from religion to genetics, from politics to modern art. I don't mean to say that Bohr was always right, but he was always thought-provoking and never trivial. How often did I cycle home through the streets of Copenhagen, intoxicated with the spirit of Platonic dialogue!*

Bohr v. Einstein: The Great Debate

Dialogue was Bohr's strong point, and in 1935 he again had an opportunity to try his skill against Einstein in their ongoing debate over the quantum theory and complementarity. In that year Einstein lodged a counterproposal, in a paper he published jointly with Boris Podolsky and Nathan Rosen (usually referred to as the EPR paper, by the last-name initials of the three authors). In this volley, Einstein, Podolsky, and Rosen argued that the quantum theory was incomplete. They proposed a thought experiment (known as the EPR experiment) to show that all objects—and quantum objects in particular—possess a physical reality that is independent of whether they are observed, measured, or disturbed in any way. This is a fundamental point of difference between classical and quantum physics. If a molecule composed of two atoms is taken, EPR argues, and the two atoms are split, sending one in one direction and the other in the other direction without disturbing their spins, it can be determined by looking at one—without looking at, measuring, or disturbing the other—what the spin of the other one is.

With a classical object this would be like taking an object such as a nickel, splitting it in half through its thickness, and mailing one half to one person and the other half to yourself. When you got your half in the mail, you would know by looking only at your half whether the other person had heads or tails.

However, in the realm of the very small, if you use two measurable variables that are connected by quantum mechanics—like momentum and position—when you measure one, you disturb the other so that it cannot be measured accurately at the same time. You can know momentum or position, but not both. Those who accept quantum theory resign themselves to this inability to know. Einstein, however, refused all such renunciations. He called this disturbance of one particle while looking at another "ghostly action at a distance." While he conceded that quantum theory did explain much, he maintained it was incomplete. Bohr offered answers to EPR, but none of them satisfied Einstein, who remained unconvinced for the rest of his life.

In 1964, after both men had died, John S. Bell brought the issue to a boil again with a general calculation for an experiment modeled on EPR, but incorporating quantum theory's restriction. He found that the probability of observing matching spins of the two separated particles was different from the probability implied by EPR. Bell's theorem created a great stir, seeming to offer proof for the quantum side of the argument. Perhaps, as Edward Speyer suggests in his book *Six Roads from Newton,* the ultimate solution will lie in interpreting parts of the setup that have not been challenged. Perhaps, like an audience at a magic show, we have been thrown off the track by letting our attention focus on the wrong part of the experiment.

Until recently, most physicists have accepted Bohr's complementarity—also known as the spirit of Copenhagen—as the only viable way to deal with the way things seem to work in the realm of the very small. In the 1980s and 1990s, however, some physicists again called Bohr's ideas about complementarity into question.

After fleeing persecution in Nazi Germany, Albert Einstein joined Princeton University's Institute for Advanced Study, with which he remained affiliated for the rest of his life. Bohr also spent some time there, and they were able to meet and continue their ongoing discussions about their thought experiments.
(Alan Richards, courtesy of the Archives, Institute for Advanced Study, Princeton, N.J.)

Science historian and physicist Philip Morrison perhaps set Bohr's contribution in the clearest light when he wrote in 1985:

> *The history of particle physics is an account of splendid successes, old and new, and of shortcomings and limitations too, to be expected in any single work of our finite species. They built a city shining upon a hill, they who half a century ago founded the quantum mechanics of particles and fields, and the design of this city is understood best through Niels Bohr.*

Tragedy and a World at War

While Bohr's work saw continued successes and challenges, for Bohr and his family in their private life, the years between 1930 and 1938 were filled with tragedy and sorrow. On Sunday morning, November 30, 1930, his mother died, after a long battle with cancer. After Ellen

Bohr's death, Niels's sister, Jenny, suffered a breakdown at the loss and was placed in a mental hospital. Two and a half years later, on May 5, 1933, she also died. Her death certificate diagnosed a state of manic depression. Niels was in Pasadena, California, at the time and heard the news by cable from Harald. Niels wrote of Jenny's warm and inspiring disposition, and both brothers felt sorrow that her illness, which she had apparently fought throughout her life, had kept her from fulfilling the potential she clearly had. When Harald spoke at her funeral, he described her as "strong in spite of her weaknesses, and healthy in spite of her illness."

On September 25, 1933, Bohr's good friend Paul Ehrenfest committed suicide. He had first met Ehrenfest in 1918, through correspondence, and they met many times and visited in each other's homes in the years that followed. But Ehrenfest, who was also friends with Einstein, had become distraught in recent years over the irreconcilable differences between Bohr and Einstein. By 1927 he said he felt he had to make a choice and sided with Bohr. By 1931 deep depression had set in. In May of that year, Bohr received a letter from him in which he said, "I have completely lost contact with theoretical physics. I cannot read anything any more and feel myself incompetent to have even the most modest grasp about what makes sense in the flood of articles and books. Perhaps I cannot at all be helped any more. Still I have the illusion that you could show me the way in a few days' encounter." But by September he wrote again to say that he was too depressed even to attend conferences.

Ehrenfest wrote a letter of desperation to Bohr, Einstein, Franck, and several other of his friends in August 1933, but he never sent it. It was found after he shot his son, Wassik, who had Down's syndrome, and himself in Amsterdam on September 25. Paul Dirac later said with great regret that he should have known that Ehrenfest was contemplating suicide, when his friend remarked to him earlier that month in Copenhagen, "Maybe, a man such as I feels he has no longer the force to live." Dirac wrote to Bohr, "I now cannot help blaming myself for not doing anything." Bohr also must have felt deep regret and sorrow at this tragic loss of a friend.

Four years later Bohr lost another close friend, his great mentor and ally Ernest Rutherford. Bohr heard the news while he was attending a conference in Bologna, Italy. Rutherford died quietly on October 19, 1937, at the age of 66, from complications following an operation for a strangulated hernia. In a talk he delivered the next day in Rutherford's memory, Bohr said, "As has been said of Galileo, . . . he left science in quite a different state from that in which he found it. . . . He will be missed more, perhaps, than any scientific worker has ever been missed before." He would also be greatly missed as a friend.

But the greatest tragedy of these years for the Bohrs occurred in July 1934. Eight years earlier, Niels had purchased a yacht, the *Chita,* with three friends, including his boyhood friend Ole Chievitz. The four had spent many joyful days sailing the waters around Denmark, setting their sails to the winds, soaking up the sun, and—with Niels on board—always discussing the application of physics to the phenomena they saw around them, from the way the sails tacked in the wind to the patterns of moonlight on the water.

On their first summer outing in 1934, Niels's 17-year-old son Christian, his oldest, was on board. It all happened very fast. The seas had been rough—certainly they had sailed before in rough waters—but on this day a huge breaker suddenly rocked the *Chita* from the port side, swinging the tiller wide and sweeping young Christian overboard. A strong swimmer, he was able to keep afloat at first, and the men threw him a life preserver. But the turbulent waters were too rough. The young man could not swim to it, and he finally disappeared beneath the waves. It was all Niels's friends could do to hold him back from jumping after his son. By that time the seas were so strong that he too would have drowned if he had attempted a rescue. Finally the *Chita* docked at a Swedish port just south of Gøteborg, and from there Niels, with great sadness, made his way to Tisvilde to tell the terrible news to Margrethe and the rest of the family. The boy's body was not found until the end of August.

Other deep difficulties loomed on the horizon. In Germany a great storm was brewing. In 1933 Hitler promulgated the first of many anti-Jewish laws, stripping "non-Aryan" academics of their posts. A great number of scientists—ultimately including more than 100 physicists—began to leave Germany.

Yet in the first 40 years of the 20th century, physics had become a hotbed of excitement. From the first amazing discoveries about radioactivity and its nature, to new ideas about the nature of the atom and the recognition that most of its mass existed at its center; from the wave-particle duality to the uncertainty principle to complementarity, the surprises never seemed to cease. Strangely, the stage, it seemed, had been set for the most astounding—"fateful," it's been said—event of all, which would take place in 1938, on the eve of World War II: the splitting of uranium atoms, which emitted further particles, which in turn could split other atoms, with the possibility of a chain reaction and the release of enormous amounts of energy.

To those who were immersed in the field of physics, the news of this unheard-of result from a laboratory near Berlin simultaneously sent two shivers down the spine: one, at the recognition of an extraordinary scientific fact—that the uranium atom could be split in this way; and a second, at the comprehension of its political implications, just as Europe was entering a war with Germany.

6

Open Door to the Nuclear Age

(1938–1945)

Of all those in the world of physics who were watching from outside Germany, Bohr was one of the first to act in response to the deepening Nazi crisis. Physicists in Germany began receiving notes from him, completely unsolicited, suggesting that they might want to come to Copenhagen to visit and discuss their plans. The subtext clearly was: I will offer you a haven and help you plan a future outside Germany. The flow of scientists from Germany to Denmark soon became steady, and, through his influence, Bohr found new positions for them in the United States, England, and Sweden.

Among those Bohr helped flee from Germany was Lise Meitner, a physicist who had been working at the Kaiser Wilhelm Institute in Berlin with the respected German chemist Otto Hahn. Meitner was also the aunt of Otto Frisch, who had escaped German rule much earlier and had been working at Bohr's institute for several years. She left Germany in 1938, and Bohr found her a position in Stockholm at the new physics laboratory the university was building there.

Lise Meitner's Insight

For 30 years, Meitner had worked side by side with Hahn, and their talents complemented each other perfectly. They were recognized as a brilliant team. An experimental chemist, Hahn typically did the laboratory work, and Meitner contributed her talents as a physics theorist to supply the theoretical analysis and interpretation of Hahn's results. Now, at 60, she was separated from both her laboratory and her partner who had stayed behind in Berlin. She had almost no equipment to work with at the not-yet-built laboratory at the new Physical Institute in Stockholm, where she had been lucky even to find a position. So when the winter holidays approached, she gladly accepted the invitation of friends to visit them on the northeast coast of Sweden in Kungälv, the little resort town where they lived.

Physicist Lise Meitner was among those whose escape from Nazi Germany through occupied Denmark to Sweden was engineered by Bohr. She learned by mail from her colleague Otto Hahn in Berlin that he thought he had achieved fission but could not believe it.
(AIP Emilio Segrè Visual Archives)

Meitner had arranged to meet her nephew Otto Frisch in this little town. He arrived to find his aunt deeply distracted and absorbed by a letter she was reading—a letter from her partner Hahn in Berlin. She barely greeted Frisch, insisting they walk and talk as she explained the letter to him. The two set out in the snow, Frisch on skis and Meitner on foot, insisting that she could keep up. The two puzzled over the letter's news, which had just arrived from Germany. The handwriting was garbled and the tone was excited. Meitner reached into her pockets and began pulling out scraps of paper to scribble out a few quick calculations.

Hahn and his assistant, Fritz Strassmann, had been trying to solve a mystery by bombarding small quantities of uranium with neutrons. This process typically produced only a few thousand atoms of "daughter substances," new substances having a different atomic makeup from the parent, which in this case was uranium. Then the challenge was to identify the new substances and explain why they were produced.

But Hahn wrote Meitner because he could not understand his results. "The fact is," he wrote, "there's something so strange about the 'radium isotopes' [produced by the bombardment] that for the time being we are mentioning it only to you. . . . Our radium isotopes act like *barium.*"

Hahn and Strassmann expected to split little pieces off the nucleus, somewhat as Rutherford had, to produce substances that were nearby on the periodic table, such as radium, with an atomic number of 88, compared with uranium's 92. Barium, however, has an atomic number of 56. As Frisch and Meitner walked, they realized that Hahn and Strassmann had done the undoable. They had split the heavy uranium atom asunder.

Both Meitner and Frisch also realized the implications of this capability in the hands of German Nazis. The relatively enormous quantity of energy released by splitting uranium atoms could have great destructive power. The conclusions they had reached, making their calculations as they sat in the snow, were also very exciting news for the scientific community. This was news that must reach the right people.

Frisch hurried back to Denmark. Arriving just before Bohr's departure by steamer for a meeting in the United States, he set the evidence before his mentor.

"Oh what idiots we all have been! Oh but this is wonderful! This is just as it must be!" exclaimed Bohr, striking his hand to his head. Excited, he encouraged his protégé to publish a paper with Meitner on their interpretation of the Hahn-Strassmann results as soon as possible. Then he embarked for the United States. En route, he mentioned the exciting news to a colleague, and at a meeting the news leaked out—before Meitner and Frisch's paper was

Heisenberg: A Question of Ethics?

In 1938, when Lise Meitner and Otto Frisch had opened the door to the nuclear age with their stunning interpretation of Hahn and Strassmann's experimental data, Germany had not yet declared war. Now, Bohr and others assumed that nuclear fission was or soon would be in the hands of the Nazi military. By September 1941, success appeared to be assured to the German cause and, in the midst of this tense, frightening scene, Werner Heisenberg traveled from Germany to occupied Denmark to pay a visit to Niels Bohr and his wife, Margrethe. The two men went for a walk as they used to do when they needed to work out issues regarding quantum mechanics and complementarity.

This time, however, things were different. Heisenberg was one of just a handful of scientists who did not flee the Nazi regime. He said (as did many other non-Nazi citizens) that he was proud of his country and its culture and wanted to stand by his homeland and help rebuild its science, which had suffered a brain drain during the 1930s when Nazi policy discriminated against Jews, banning them from public institutions such as universities and institutes. Heisenberg advanced to an administrative position in Leipzig and then became director of the Kaiser Wilhelm Institute for Physics.

Heisenberg's supporters point out that he was not the enemy. During 1937, he had suffered the scrutiny of the Nazi SS, who accused Heisenberg of teaching "Jewish physics," a name they used to attack the teaching of modern theoretical physics because of its connection with Einstein and other Jewish physicists. They also called him a "white Jew." He underwent a year-long Gestapo investigation that was daunting and frightening, but he was eventually exonerated by SS Heinrich Himmler himself and was deemed loyal.

No one knows what Heisenberg and Bohr discussed or what Heisenberg's goal was when he made the trip to Copenhagen. He had accepted the position of scientific director of the German nuclear project and was working at the time on a fission reactor, for the purpose, he said, of providing atomic power (not a bomb). However, he later claimed that he had believed the project required tons of pure uranium-235 to work and he never completed the calculation to find out what it might require to make a bomb.

Was Heisenberg working on an atomic bomb? Was he trying to throw Nazi engineers and scientists off the trail to success with fission and the bomb? Or was his failure to produce a bomb just a mistake?

Werner Heisenberg and Bohr were friends and colleagues before World War II, as shown in this picture, but the ties grew uncomfortable when Heisenberg did not leave Germany. Many feared he was working on the atomic bomb. (Paul Ehrenfast, Jr., courtesy AIP Emilio Segrè Visual Archives, Weisskopf Collection)

What did he want from Bohr? Was he fishing for information about whether the Allied forces were working on a bomb and what progress they had made so far? Was he working for the Nazi government, trying to persuade Bohr (as he had already tried to do in other occupied countries) that living under German rule was not so bad?

No one knows what was said, but, by the time the two physicists finished their conversation on that occasion, Bohr was clearly upset and the relationship would never recover. After carefully considering all the available documents and evidence (including several unsent letters written by Bohr to Heisenberg), science historian David C. Cassidy has concluded that Heisenberg wanted Bohr to exert the pressure of his influence on Allied scientists to get them to back off from working on the bomb. "Bohr," says Cassidy, "to his credit, immediately sensed Heisenberg's intentions and broke off the conversation."

published, as it turned out (a slipup that Bohr always regretted). Literally overnight, physicists and chemists in universities all over the United States began testing the premise and found it was true. The atom had been split! The worlds of physics and chemistry had been flipped upside-down.

Bohr, of course, was devastated that he had leaked a discovery by other scientists before they had a chance to publish, and rushed to write a note for publication in explanation.

The ultimate result of Hahn and Strassmann's experimental results, which would have been published (and were) in any case, was that the United States and Great Britain decided to build an atomic bomb, out of fear of this knowledge in German hands.

Escape

In 1940 the German threat moved closer for Bohr, when the German armies invaded his homeland. He and Margrethe decided to stay, however, and in the following three years, he became prominent in efforts to get those in danger out of Denmark, helping them find boats to cross the sea to safety.

Another concern of Bohr's, of course, was that assets and equipment should be prevented from falling into German hands, if possible. Bohr devised a means to protect two Nobel medals—Max Planck's and Max Laue's—that had been given to him for safekeeping. To prevent the Nazis from recognizing the value of the medals, he dissolved them in acid and hid the acid-filled vials. After the war he precipitated the gold out of the acid and recast the medals in their original form for return to their owners. (Bohr had donated his own medal to aid the Finnish war effort.)

Bohr stayed in Denmark until 1943, when it became clear that the Germans intended to imprison him. He and his family narrowly escaped in a fishing boat, and once he reached safety in Sweden he continued to help many others escape. There the decision was made to fly him with his son Aage, then 21, to London, where they could help with the British war effort. Bundled into the cramped bomb bay of an unarmed Mosquito British bomber, Bohr became preoccupied during the flight and pushed off his helmet. Bohr didn't hear the pilot's

Copenhagen, the Play

The unexplained September 1941 meeting between Werner Heisenberg and Niels Bohr in Copenhagen continues to call up many questions of intent, potential compromise, and personal relationship. The famous meeting was the focus of a drama called *Copenhagen* that played in London to sold-out audiences in 1998, then opened a short time later in New York to enthusiastic acclaim.

The play, written by Michael Frayn, relies on only three characters to carry its probing dialogue and questioning narrative. The three players are the ghosts of Heisenberg, Bohr, and Bohr's wife, Margrethe, the three people who were there that sad day when Heisenberg came to the Bohr home. The three ghosts return to the big house, now deserted, to replay a series of possible scenarios for the meeting. The story is told using the different viewpoints of each character, evenhandedly, leaving no one character carrying the burden of guilt. Nothing is really resolved, but the play raises questions still valid, still unanswered—and that is the reason, according to science historian David C. Cassidy, a Heisenberg biographer, that today's audiences find the play powerful and thought provoking.

Cassidy states his discomfort, though, with the broad but relatively shallow issues explored in *Copenhagen*. The play looks at questions about nuclear fission that apparently puzzled Heisenberg, it touches on the controversies raised by quantum, and the family concerns they shared as friends.

Where are the big issues, Cassidy queries? How could a nation imbued with a fine culture and composed of intelligent, well-educated people possibly have crushed out the lives of millions of people in the most deadly genocide of the century? How could Heisenberg—a talented, creative, brilliant physicist, educated in the best traditions of Northern Europe—have agreed to support Nazi Germany?

Instead, these questions form a background wallpaper to the issues that are explored by *Copenhagen*: Why did Heisenberg come to Copenhagen? What did he want to convey to Bohr? What did he, in turn, want from Bohr?

No one knows the answers to these questions because no one else went on the walk the two of them took together. No one else heard what they said. One thing is certain, however. The conversation that day shook Bohr, and the close friendship and collaborative teamwork between Bohr and Heisenberg would never recover.

warning that they would be flying to high altitude, and by the time the plane arrived in London, he was near death from lack of oxygen.

Physicists Called to Battle

Niels and Aage journeyed to the United States in late 1943 as representatives of the British. There security authorities were anxious to keep the bomb-building Manhattan Project as secret as possible—the psychological power of an unexpected attack potentially was an even mightier weapon than the bomb itself. They worried that the Bohrs' presence in the United States might be noticed and questioned and that some comment in a newspaper might tip spies off to the existence of the project. So, on arrival, officials issued false identification papers to Niels and Aage, disguising Niels as "Mr. Nicholas Baker," and his son as "James Baker." (Niels, of course, forgot that his real name was inscribed on his suitcase!) Throughout their travels they were accompanied by an armed bodyguard, complete with signed receipts for their well-being required at every changing of the guard.

Under guard, the two proceeded circuitously to a pine-dotted mesa called Los Alamos in northern New Mexico. There the United States government had gathered the best physicists in the country to work on a secret project—the development of the atomic bomb. Aage, whom everyone called "Jim," became a junior scientific officer, and Niels ("Uncle Nick") became consultant to the directorate, headed by Robert Oppenheimer, a tall, lean man who also smoked a pipe and whose intelligence and energy radiated in Los Alamos as Niels's did in Copenhagen.

"Bohr at Los Alamos was marvelous," Oppenheimer would later say in a lecture after the war. "He took a very lively technical interest . . . But his real function, I think for almost all of us, was not the technical one. He made the enterprise which looked so macabre seem hopeful."

In later reflections, Oppenheimer defined Bohr's vision as a kind of complementarity of the bomb—a weapon of great destruction that, unused, could be the key to a different world. He brought this message to the scientists at Los Alamos. Victor Weisskopf, a young physicist who had fled from Austria and worked at Los Alamos, would later describe Bohr's contribution in these terms:

In Los Alamos we were working on something which is perhaps the most questionable, the most problematic thing a scientist can be faced with. At that time physics, our beloved science, was pushed into the most cruel part of reality and we had to live it through. We were, most of us at least, young and somewhat inexperienced in human affairs, I would say. But suddenly in the midst of it, Bohr appeared in Los Alamos.

It was the first time we became aware of the sense in all these terrible things, because Bohr right away participated not only in the work, but in our discussions. Every great and deep difficulty bears in itself its own solution . . . This we learned from him.

By mid-February 1944, Bohr was back in Washington, where he contacted a friend who was a justice of the U.S. Supreme Court, Felix Frankfurter. Through carefully circumspect communication, they established that they both were aware of Los Alamos and the Manhattan Project. Through Frankfurter, Bohr communicated with President Roosevelt about his concerns regarding the postwar future. From the communications from Roosevelt, Frankfurter and Bohr decided that the president wanted Bohr to act as go-between to Winston Churchill, prime minister of Britain, to express the president's concern and his interest in including the Soviets among those informed about the bomb project. The idea was that if the United States and Britain confided in the

J. Robert Oppenheimer headed the secret Manhattan Project, the Allied forces' successful effort to build an atomic bomb in Los Alamos, New Mexico.
(J. Robert Oppenheimer Memorial Committee)

While visiting Los Alamos, Bohr skied the snowy slopes, all the while thinking and talking about atomic physics.
(John P. Miller, courtesy AIP Emilio Segrè Visual Archives, Segrè Collection)

Soviets early, postwar arms control might result, whereas failure to include the Soviets would almost certainly lead to an arms race.

Niels and Aage went to London, apparently with a mandate to talk with the prime minister, and on May 16 Niels set out for 10 Downing Street. Aage, who was Niels's complete confidante and acted as his secretary during this period, remembered what happened in this way:

> *We came to London full of hopes and expectations. It was, of course, a rather novel situation that a scientist should thus try to intervene in world politics, but it was hoped that Churchill, who possessed such imagination and who had often shown such great vision, would be inspired by the new prospects.*

The meeting went very badly. Churchill was in a bad mood, suspected his aides of subterfuge, and barely gave Bohr an opportunity to talk. When Bohr asked if he could write to Churchill, the prime minister replied, "It will be an honour for me to receive a letter from you, but not about politics." According to some sources, Churchill became so angry over the incident that he nearly had Bohr arrested.

Discouraged but unstoppable, Bohr did write to Churchill and to Roosevelt, several times, and also returned to the United States to communicate again with Roosevelt through his contact, Frankfurter. But Churchill failed to recognize that the bomb would not remain a secret forever, that if the British and Americans could build an atomic bomb, so could other nations, and that, as Bohr would put it succinctly in later life, "We are in a completely new situation that cannot be resolved by war."

7

The Final Years

1945–1962

Germany surrendered in May 1945, and for Europe the war was finally over. But war continued to rage in the Pacific, and the development of the atomic bomb was coming to a climax in Los Alamos. On July 16, 1945, the first detonation of a nuclear device occurred in a test explosion at nearby Trinity. On August 6 Hiroshima was destroyed by an atomic bomb at 8:15 A.M., Japanese time. On August 9 a second bomb was dropped, this time striking Nagasaki. It was 11:02 A.M., Japanese time.

Public Life: Search for a Better World

Two days later an article written by Niels Bohr with Aage's help appeared in the London *Times.* Its title was "Science and Civilization," and it was Bohr's first public plea for a world where open exchange of information could prevent such horrors in the future. He wrote:

> *Civilization is presented with a challenge more serious perhaps than ever before. . . . We have reached the stage where the degree of security offered to the citizens of a nation by collective defense measures is entirely insufficient. . . . No control can be effective without free access to full scientific information and the granting of the opportunity of international supervision of all undertakings which, unless regulated, might become a source of disaster. . . . The contribution which an agreement about this vital matter would make . . . can hardly be exaggerated.*

Niels and Margrethe Bohr returned home to Copenhagen at last on August 25, where they resumed their life at Carlsberg House and Tisvilde. Bohr, as always, threw himself headlong into his work and enjoyed the company of his grandchildren, for whom he loved to buy toys and gadgets. In some ways his life went on as before; in some ways it was greatly changed.

By 1945, Niels Bohr had become an eminent public figure, not only in Denmark, but worldwide. The king and queen of Denmark came to Carlsberg House for dinner, as did cabinet ministers and ambassadors. A lengthy procession of high dignitaries and heads of state paid visits to Bohr in Copenhagen during the years following the war—including Queen Elizabeth II and Prince Philip of England, the queen of Siam, the crown prince of Japan, the prime ministers of India and Israel, and even Winston Churchill, the man who almost had him thrown in prison during the war. As always, he also entertained a steady parade of physicists, both senior and junior, and spent long hours talking to them and listening to their ideas.

At 60, Bohr's energy had not flagged—he still took the steps at the institute two at a time. He continued his involvement with research issues as well as the continuing growth of the institute. But also, in the years following the war, he became more and more involved in an issue that had come to trouble him greatly ever since the specter of the atomic bomb had become visible.

Even before the war drew to a close, as the Allies gained the upper hand, Bohr had constantly looked ahead, recognizing the future of distrust, fear, and possible destruction that the world's nations would face after the war. Although the Allies had cooperated well during the war, he knew that the spirit of cooperation would not be maintained once the current threat was past. Too many fundamental differences in economic and political organization existed among them. He had seen firsthand how difficult it was even to maintain scientific contacts with colleagues within the Soviet Union, as that vast Communist country grew more and more isolated. And he could foretell that finding a basis for cooperation between East and West would be a monumental, if not impossible, task.

As Aage Bohr later explained:

> *It was against this background that my father saw the prospects of the atom bomb, and he realized immediately how decisively this new development would affect the world. He perceived that soon the world might be faced with an arms race that would threaten the continued existence of civilization itself. However, it was characteristic of my father's whole attitude that he also saw immediately that these very prospects offered new possibilities of giving political developments a more favourable turn. Indeed, everyone would have to realize that the world was changed for better or for worse, that now a comprehensive and genuine co-operation was necessary to avoid living under the most ominous threats. Here was a vital task for united effort.*

During the coming decade, Bohr made use of his many contacts, working tirelessly for his vision of a better world—a world where the threat of atomic weapons was defused by a policy of worldwide openness. He continued to make overtures to governments. In 1948 he met with George Marshall, the secretary of state of the United States. Marshall listened with interest, but, in the end, the U.S. government balked at backing Bohr's policy.

By August 1949, the Soviet Union had exploded its first test bomb. The United States made a public announcement in 1950 that it would pursue development of the hydrogen bomb. The arms race Bohr had feared had begun.

Letter to the United Nations

But Bohr would not give up. He decided to make a direct worldwide appeal, no longer in private conferences with heads of state but in an open letter to the United Nations. In February 1950 he arrived

Considered one of the greatest theoretical physicists since Sir Isaac Newton, Bohr was an inspired theorist, a charismatic teacher and leader, and a compassionate humanitarian. (Max Planck Institute fur Physik, courtesy AIP Emilio Segrè Visual Archives)

once again for a short stay at the Institute for Advanced Study in Princeton, where he enlisted the help of his former student and future biographer, Abraham Pais. Many discussions ensued. Bohr returned to Copenhagen in May, where he and Harald hammered out the text of the letter in secret. They sent the letter to Bohr's son Aage, who at the time was at Columbia University in New York. At 10:00 A.M. on June 9, a moment timed to coincide with a press conference Bohr called in Copenhagen, Aage Bohr delivered the letter to the office of the secretary general of the United Nations, Trygve Lie.

The following excerpt contains the major points of the letter:

> *The situation calls for the most unprejudiced attitude towards all questions of international relations. Indeed, proper appreciation of the duties and responsibilities implied in world citizenship is in our time more necessary than ever before. On the one hand, the progress of science and technology has tied the fate of all nations inseparably together, on the other hand, it is on a most different cultural background that vigorous endeavours for national self-assertion and social development are being made in the various parts of our globe. An open world where each nation can assert itself solely by the extent to which it can contribute to the common culture and is able to help others with experience and resources must be the goal to be put above everything else . . . The arguments presented suggest that every initiative from any side towards the removal of obstacles for free mutual information and intercourse would be of the greatest importance in breaking the present deadlock and encouraging others to take steps in the same direction.*

Bohr opened his press conference in Copenhagen and read the contents of his letter before the assembled members of the press. Having said everything he meant to say in the text of some 5,500 words, he refused, for the most part, to accept questions and concluded his news conference.

The reaction was disappointing. Secretary General Lie acknowledged receiving the letter, assuring Bohr that he would give it most careful consideration, but the international body never made plans to discuss or debate its premises. Few outside the Scandinavian countries paid any attention to the news conference. Not until Bohr distributed thousands of copies (printed at his own expense) to the foreign news media, heads of state, colleagues, and friends did some feedback begin to drift in. But even then the response was primarily neutral or negative.

Two of the more positive reactions came from the *Washington Post* and the *New York Herald Tribune.* The first cautioned somewhat lamely against dismissing Bohr's ideas without some consideration. The New York paper maintained, only a little more supportively, "The open world is an idea of such simplicity, such power and such potential effect that it is not lightly to be dismissed."

The times were not right for the kind of trust and mutual cooperation that Bohr envisioned, and would not be for another 30 years. Instead, June 24 of 1954 marked the beginning of the Korean War, and the United States exploded its first hydrogen (thermonuclear) bomb in the Pacific before the year was out.

Bohr never gave up on his idea, though. During the last 20 years of his life, he focused primarily on the problems as well as the prospects inherent in the release of atomic energy. And he always continued to maintain that openness—free access to information and free exchange of ideas—was the only course that would be in the mutual interest of all nations.

A fine footnote to this period of Bohr's life came about in 1985 long after his death, when Mikhail Gorbachev came to power in the Soviet Union, promoting what he called glasnost, a new spirit of openness between his country and the West. That fall, all Denmark celebrated the centenary of Bohr's birth, and among the several special events that took place in Copenhagen, a three-way TV hookup was arranged, linking speakers in Copenhagen, Moscow, and Cambridge, Massachusetts, to discuss the challenge of nuclear armaments. Afterward, a book of essays was published on the subject, "dedicated to Niels Bohr and his appeal for an open world."

Physicists, Particle Physics, Openness, and Peace

Bohr had appealed for political action to turn atomic energy to human benefit, with no results; thereafter he turned to the scientific community. Physics, he argued, could lay the groundwork of cooperation between nations. During the 1950s he became involved in several international projects that have greatly advanced the study of physics in Europe. By this time physics had entered a new phase, with particle physics replacing nuclear physics as the cutting edge of the field. Particle physics, sometimes referred to as "high-energy" physics, took another step deeper into the mysteries of the atom. Theoretical and experimental investigations of subatomic particles required powerful (high-energy) machines, far bigger and more expensive than the accelerators of the 1930s. Clearly, if European nations wanted to recover from the "brain drain" caused by the departure of thousands of German and Italian scientists during the war, cooperation was necessary.

In part as a result of discussions at a conference in Copenhagen called by Bohr in 1951, the idea developed for a new, international center for theoretical and experimental physics. By 1952 representatives from 14 European countries met in Copenhagen to lay the groundwork for the *Conseil Européen pour la Recherche Nucléaire* (European Council for Nuclear Research), known as CERN. The cooperation, of course, did not go completely smoothly. Debates ensued about what kind of equipment was needed and where it should be located. Bohr and others had hoped that CERN might locate in Copenhagen, and for a time the theoretical branch was located there. But in the end, Geneva became the chosen site, and by 1957 a synchrocyclotron particle accelerator operating at 0.6 giga electron volts (0.6 GeV, or 1 billion electron volts) was in operation. By 1959 the proton synchrotron particle accelerator began operating at 28 GeV.

When it became clear that CERN would not stay in Copenhagen, Bohr helped organize a theoretical physics consortium, not in competition with CERN, formed jointly by an alliance of Scandinavian countries, including Denmark, Norway, and Sweden. Called Nordita (for *Nordisk Institut for Theoretisk Atomfysik*), the new institute would be centered in Copenhagen. Finland joined the group in 1955. Nordita began operations on September 1, 1957, much to Bohr's pleasure. In 1964, after Bohr's death, Nordita moved into quarters next to the Institute for Theoretical Physics. (Bohr's institute was renamed the Niels Bohr Institute the following year.) With expanded research programs in both institutes—including condensed matter physics, particle physics, and astrophysics—today the two institutes work closely together. Nordita has thrived in the more than 35 years since its foundation, having become a center for research, colloquiums, and conferences that attract participants from all over the world.

A third opportunity came to light in December 1953, when President Dwight D. Eisenhower made a proposal before the United Nations, calling for an end to the atomic arms race and establishment of international cooperation to promote peaceful uses for atomic energy. While this proposal sounds like more than it was (the arms race did not come to an end), Eisenhower was implying that uranium sources might be made available to other countries. Denmark was among the first to express interest. The Danish Academy of Technical Sciences was instrumental in getting the ball rolling. A committee took form, chaired by Bohr, and in 1954 Bohr visited with the prime minister of Denmark to explore the possibility with him. In March 1955 the government formed a Preparatory Atomic Energy Commission, with Bohr at its head. Beginning in April 1955, Bohr began working on arrangements with the Danish government for establishing agreements with the United States and the United Kingdom for technical consultation on the building and construction of reactors.

Meanwhile, he began searching for a suitable site for the reactors and research facility, in many cases personally checking out possible islands and peninsulas. Finally he asked a group of commission members to take a look at a couple of sites he thought had potential. The spot he was considering was located near the medieval city of Roskilde, about 20 miles west of Copenhagen. The first site, which he thought was the less likely of the two, was an island, called Bolund, that at low tide nearly formed a peninsula. One of the commissioners told of the excursion in wonder:

> *We went down to the beach. From there it seemed evident that it did not suit the purpose. Bohr was not content with guesses, however. We should have a look. Off with shoes and socks, up with pants, out into the water, Bohr ahead, over sharp stones, then up the slope to Bolund's top—our guess was correct, we could in good conscience drop Bolund and concentrate on*

other possibilities—in the meantime we had learned something about Bohr's working style.

By the following year Denmark was ready to set up a permanent Atomic Energy Commission, and Bohr was asked to accept the chairmanship, which he gladly did. He was 70 years old. A rocky peninsula called Risø, which jutted out into the fjord near the rejected island of Bolund, would be the site, and by the fall of 1956, construction on the research laboratories had begun. Contracts were signed to acquire three reactors. By the summer of 1957, laboratories for physics, chemistry, reactor development, and electronics were in use. A machine shop, meteorology station, and agricultural station were also in operation. A formal inauguration ceremony took place on June 6, 1958 with the king and queen of Denmark and many other Danish and foreign officials in attendance. By 1960 all three reactors were in full operation.

Under Bohr's direction, facilities at the Institute for Theoretical Physics were growing as well. A new five-story building was under construction, and an underground structure to house the revamped cyclotron was built. In addition, the institute scientists felt that a larger accelerator was needed—but there was no place left to build in the area surrounding the institute. The Atomic Energy Commission came to the rescue with an offer of land near the Risø center. Plans for building a new laboratory began at once, with an accelerator that could produce protons at 10 to 12 MeV (million electron volts)—only a fraction the size of the accelerator at the new CERN facility, but nonetheless an exciting prospect for physics research in Denmark. It first went into operation in 1961. The new laboratory is now called the Niels Bohr Institute, like the institute in Copenhagen, and it has become a vital nexus of international research.

Although Bohr's well-considered, even noble, plea for openness among nations went virtually unheeded in the political arena, he had clearly succeeded in marshaling international cooperation among scientists and in developing peaceful uses for the release of atomic energy. On October 24, 1957 the first Atoms for Peace Award—a gold medal and a check for $75,000—was presented to him at the Great Hall of the National Academy of Sciences in Washington, D.C. At that time President Eisenhower called Bohr "a great man whose mind has explored the mysteries of the inner structure of atoms, and whose spirit has reached into the very heart of man."

Between 1945 and 1961 Bohr delivered more than 20 lectures all over the world. In the process, he also received more than 30 honorary doctorates from such prestigious institutions as Princeton and Columbia universities. During the 1950s Bohr's travels were extensive, including visits to Iceland in 1951, to Israel in 1953, to Yugoslavia in 1956, to Greenland in 1957, and again to Yugoslavia and Israel in 1958.

Shrinking Circle of Friends

Bohr also made numerous visits to the United States, usually spending time in residence at the Institute for Advanced Study in Princeton, where he had a standing membership. During his visits of February to June 1948, February to May 1950, and September to December 1954, he often camped in Einstein's office (Einstein preferred the office anteroom or the study at his home) and held forth in his continuing discussion with his old friend, always trying to swing him over to his own way of thinking about complementarity and quantum mechanics. He never succeeded.

Einstein's death in April 1955 hit Bohr hard. This was a friend for whom he had the deepest respect, admiration, and love. His inability to reconcile their intellectual differences gnawed at him constantly, and Einstein was on his mind for the rest of his life. In a memorial, Bohr wrote, "With the death of Albert Einstein, a life in the service of science and humanity which was as fruitful as any in the whole history of our culture has come to an end . . . He gave us a world picture with a unity and harmony surpassing the boldest dreams of the past." But for Bohr personally, much more than that, a kindred mind, a sort of twin light had gone out. "To the whole of mankind Albert Einstein's death is a great loss and to those of us who had the good fortune to enjoy his warm friendship it is a grief that we shall nevermore be able to see his gentle smile and listen to him."

Bohr suffered two other great personal losses during the 1950s. In 1951 his brother, Harald, died of cancer at the age of 63. Next to his wife, Harald had always been Niels's closest friend and greatest ally. The loss was huge. Seven years later, in 1958, Wolfgang Pauli died suddenly in Zurich, Switzerland. Of all the younger physicists Bohr had worked with in the 1920s and 1930s, Pauli had always understood him most intuitively. Niels and Margrethe traveled to Switzerland for the memorial services.

As his 75th birthday approached, Bohr traveled to India in January 1960, where he attended the Indian Science Congress in Bombay. There he delivered two lectures, on human knowledge and atoms, and on the principles of quantum physics. He took time to explore Calcutta, Madras, Agra, and Delhi, where he visited with the prime minister, Jawaharlal Nehru. He and Margrethe also visited the carved caves of Elephanta in Bombay Harbor, known for their eighth-century sculptured figures, as well as the caves of Ellora in central India and Ajanta in east-central India, known for their exquisite ancient sculptures, carvings, and paintings, some dating back as far as the third century B.C.

The following month he journeyed to Geneva for the inauguration of CERN, and in May of 1961 he visited the Soviet Union for the second time, where he stopped at institutions in Moscow and Dubna and spent three days in Georgia.

But by the fall of 1961, Niels Bohr was finally beginning to slow down. At the 12th Solvay conference in Brussels that October—the 50th anniversary of the first of these meetings—he presented a talk entitled "The Solvay Meetings and the Development of Quantum Physics." He asked permission to deliver the address from his seat.

Still, in June 1962 Bohr made another short trip to the United States to accept an honorary doctorate from the Rockefeller Institute in New York, and later that month he drove with Margrethe by car from Copenhagen to Cologne, Germany, where he delivered a talk entitled "Light and Life Revisited" at the opening of the Institute of Genetics. Throughout his career, Bohr had at various times tried to apply complementarity and a mechanistic approach to biology, an effort that was rarely well received. On this occasion, he stated, in a typical effort to reset humanity's sights on the search for truth: "In the last resort, it is a matter of how one makes headway in biology. . . . Life will always be a wonder, but what changes is the balance between the feeling of wonder and the courage to try to understand."

From Cologne, the Bohrs continued on to the Bavarian city of Lindau, located on Lake Constance, where Nobel laureates traditionally gathered annually. While there Niels suddenly became ill. He was hospitalized with a diagnosis of minor cerebral hemorrhage and then was hurried back to receive medical attention in Denmark. He spent the following month recuperating with Margrethe at Tisvilde, where the two celebrated their golden wedding anniversary on August 1. It was a joyful party, attended by all the children and grandchildren—in whom Bohr always delighted enormously.

On September 30, Margrethe and Niels left for Italy, where they spent a happy vacation together in the resort town of Amalfi, overlooking the Gulf of Salerno on the southwestern coast. The sunlight sparkled on the azure waters, and the air smelled of fresh lemons and sea breezes, as colorful fishing boats bobbed in the little port. There they relaxed and celebrated Niels's 77th birthday, returning to Copenhagen on October 27.

With his doctor's blessing, Bohr resumed his regular work schedule, chairing a meeting of the Danish Royal Academy of Sciences and Literature on Friday, November 16, 1962, as he had for many years. The following day he kept an appointment to tape an interview on the history of quantum physics. His voice sounded tired.

November 18, 1962, was a Sunday, and after lunching with Margrethe and a few friends, Bohr went upstairs to take a nap. A few moments later his wife heard him call out "Margrethe," and she rushed up the stairs to his side. Niels had collapsed, unconscious, next to his bed. The diagnosis was heart failure.

Niels Bohr's remains were cremated, and burial took place at Assistens Kirkegaard, where his ashes were placed near those he loved best—his brother Harald, his son Christian, and his parents. Twenty-two years later his wife, Margrethe, was buried at his side.

Niels Bohr and the Pursuit of Truth

The public reaction to Bohr's death was a great outpouring of admiration, respect, and affection. Physicists and friends from all over the world sent their condolences. In an unprecedented tribute to a nonmember, the *Folketing* (the Danish parliament) stood to honor him as their president talked of Denmark's sorrow. The prime minister of Israel, the king of Sweden, the chancellor of Germany, and President Kennedy of the United States all sent messages. Newspapers and magazines bore tributes such as "With the passing of Niels Bohr the world has lost not only one of the great scientists of this century but also one of the intellectual giants of all time" (the *New York Times*). And "For physicists throughout the world, Niels Bohr, the gentle genius of Denmark, has long embodied the heroic image of a scientist" (the *Christian Science Monitor*).

But perhaps the greatest representation of Niels Bohr's untiring effort to pursue knowledge remained untouched on his study blackboard—a diagram drawn the night before his death in one last effort to overcome the arguments of his longtime friend and intellectual sparring partner, Albert Einstein.

Bohr's bulldog tenacity in the long-standing debate, of course, was not one-sided. A month before Einstein's death, Einstein was also still writing about his disagreements with the Copenhagen interpretation and Bohr's arguments.

And the debate isn't over yet. Today a few physicists still have problems with what they call the "Copenhagen orthodoxy" and have begun to veer away from using Bohr's complementarity to explain the physical characteristics of the atom. If they are on the right track, Bohr would be the first to rejoice. As Otto Frisch once wrote about him, "He never hesitated for a moment to admit that he had been in error; to him it merely meant that he now understood things better, and what could have made him happier?"

Albert Einstein once said of Bohr, "He utters his opinions like one perpetually groping and never like one who believes to be in possession of definite truth." For a scientist, this was the ultimate compliment, from one of the greatest scientists of all time. It was this quality, above all, that made Niels Bohr the remarkable scientist that he was and a supreme model for anyone who is truly committed to the pursuit of truth.

8

Rethinking Bohr's Physics

The early years of the 20th century framed an exciting period in physics as experimentalists and theoreticians tried to reconcile the consequences of each new discovery—Becquerel and radiation, the Curies and their discovery of radium, emerging theories about the nature of the atom, including Ernest Rutherford and chemist Frederick Soddy's 1902 paper on transformation, or, even more daring, transmutation of radioactive elements. Talk like that felt uncomfortably like alchemy, long known to be a pseudoscience. However, the data were there, teased out one by one in Rutherford's best ground-solid, carefully documented experimental technique. Many scientists, including Marie Curie, rejected the idea that one element might decay into another. But transformation theory fit in place like exactly the right piece in a jigsaw puzzle. (No alchemy involved, of course.) Transformation theory made the newly discovered radioactive substances far easier to explain, and most scientists were convinced that it was essentially correct. However, questions began to well up about what caused radioactive decay and why this apparent randomness entered into the customarily well-ordered world of physics. What happened to cause and effect?

Then came quantum mechanics, with its many unexpected conclusions. Physics was on the edge of the greatest revolution since Isaac Newton's work on gravity and light in the 17th century. A new vision of the universe began to emerge. As Max Born recognized, cause and effect worked in the macro-sized physical reality of Newtonian physics, but in the microworld probability reigned. You could not pronounce the status caused by a crash in the world of quantum mechanics—only a statement of probability is possible: "How probable is a given effect of the collision?" One new concept rolled quickly into the next, in an explosion of keen thinking, teamwork, and creativity. It was in this environment that Heisenberg came up with the now-famous uncertainty principle—the recognition that you *can* know one thing or another but not *both.*

During the later years of his life, Einstein became interested in the idea of a single theory, a sort of mother of all monster theories, a TOE—an all-purpose "Theory of Everything" that would address all the contradictions and paradoxes that lived in the world of quantum mechanics. By the end of Niels Bohr's lifetime, physics was moving more and more toward Einstein's quest for a universal theory—a TOE. So far, the most promising of these efforts has been a strange set of ideas known as string theory, or, rather, the brand most physicists subscribe to today is called superstring theory. Physicists have spent three decades serving up this brew, and, while many aspects of this theory seem to fit, much of it is very strange and not so easy to take. Superstrings have so completely taken over in the macroworld, while still being difficult to understand, that some physicists and mathematicians are beginning to wonder what happens if they are wrong? Nobel physicist Murray Gell-Mann liked to call string theory "the only game in town." That is, no one has come up with any other theory that can even begin to explain the universe as well as string theory. It is admittedly promising. String theory brings together Einstein's relativity and the same quantum mechanics that fascinated Bohr, Heisenberg, Pauli, and all the rest. Further, it explains the tiny particles of fundamental physics. They are not "pointlike," Martin Gardner explains in an April 2007 book review. Strings are formed by superfine filaments of energy so tiny that they cannot be seen or otherwise detected, even by using a collider.

What Are Strings?

Strings may either have two ends or form a closed loop, sort of like a broken rubber band of the sort that comes with the Sunday paper—but not really, because strings are pure energy and have only one dimension, and their universe is partly recognizable as our universe but does not stop with the space-time continuum as we know it, with its three spatial dimensions and time. Strings live in that universe and they make it hum. That is, they live in a space composed of those four dimensions plus six or seven more that are "compacted." Far smaller than any atomic particle, strings are staggeringly tiny: a millionth of a billionth of a billionth of a billionth of a centimeter. These minuscule forms are attached to every point in our four dimensions that make up space and time (or spacetime). They have a tough job: The vibration and movement of the strings create the very fabric of space itself, along with all of nature's fundamental forces and elementary particles.

In the 30 years since the first introduction of string theory into the world of physics, thousands of papers and dissertations have been written about string theory. Although many physicists rejected string theory at first as improbable, it has become much more respectable in recent years.

The Universe Both Big and Small

The great search for Bohr—and other theoretical physicists from Newton to today—was to find the best description of nature, the one that best captured the essence of reality and existence. The very enormity of the universe defies our ability to understand, but physicists have found that the tools of mathematics go far toward enabling humans to find ways to explain the place where we live.

Newton used calculus to describe motion mathematically, and physicists who followed him were able to extend his model for the gravitational force to the science and technology of electromagnetism. As calculus evolved to become classical field theory, many scientists felt that they had arrived at the best description of nature possible. They had gone as far as possible, they believed. They had done the job and nothing remained to explain or describe.

Then J. J. Thomson discovered the electron and particle physics was off and running. This was the heyday of Niels Bohr and his colleagues. Quantum mechanics and experimental observation provided the toeholds for finding and describing atomic particles, and, by using mathematical and conceptual tools provided by Bohr, Einstein, and others who followed them, physicists deduced that all particles fell into two categories: fermions or bosons. Bosons are particles that transmit forces, and many bosons can occupy the same state at the same time. But not fermions. Only one fermion can occupy the same state at the same time. So fermions are the particles that make up matter. This is why solids do not pass through each other, which one might expect them to do, given the way atoms are built. Due to this phenomenon, known as Pauli repulsion, fermions (matter) cannot share the same space the way bosons can.

As particle physics developed with quantum mechanics, Einstein was providing ways to understand how light works. In his special theory of relativity, he developed mathematics that helped him describe and model this phenomenon. Combined with the later development of quantum mechanics, relativistic quantum field theory was born. Therein would lay the groundwork used by theoretical physicists of the last half of the 20th century to describe and explore the behavior of subatomic particles—even smaller than particles.

Einstein's legacy did not stop there. He extended his special theory of relativity to include Newton's theory of gravitation—giving birth to the general theory of relativity. This formulation of gravity shows that space and time communicate the gravitational force through their curvature—and this view of how things work has served well to help describe nature. Sometimes it has left both scientists and the public in awe with its generally unexpected explanations, for example when it predicted the existence of black holes and when it successfully showed that the universe was expanding.

The Impossible Dream?

Since the heyday of the particle physicists, however, string theory has taken over the forward pursuit of understanding the complexities of the natural world we live in. Going back again to the incredibly small, these tiny filaments called strings seem to explain much about the universe in mathematical terms. Superstring theory is founded on three key ideas: a principle called supersymmetry; the existence of additional dimensions; and the manifestation of gravity as a force defined by the exchange of quantum particles. However, even after 30 years of study, no experiment has ever succeeded in showing that strings—or string theory's three claims to existence—actually exist.

Supersymmetry is a mathematical principle that allows force-carrying particles, such as photons and gluons, to transform into each other. If supersymmetry exists, theoreticians envision that every particle has an unseen shadow partner that is very large (too large for colliders to help with the job of finding them). The prospect of multiverses—multiple universes—intrigues many physicists and the public as well. According to physicist Sten Odenwald, with the existence of string theory's six or seven hidden dimensions, trillions of possible six-dimensional geometries would exist and each one would call up its own, unique universe. However, if either one of these conditions do not exist, then string theory is no longer viable and 30 years of work since Bohr's time would be useless and theoretical physics would have to revert to the standard model. More uncertainty exists. Physicists have also come to depend on string theory for explaining astronomical features such as dark matter, dark energy, and cosmic inflation.

Looking back to Bohr's time, the journey through decades of string theory seems intriguing, even compelling, but many theorists are beginning to wonder "What if . . . ?"

Conclusion:

The Legacy of Niels Bohr

When Niels Bohr died on November 18, 1962, a great light went out, the illuminations of a brilliant and humane mind were stilled, and, as many sadly put it at the time, the last of the great giants had gone.

Even more than Einstein, Niels Bohr had created new ways of looking at the world in the first half of the 20th century. With the Bohr atom, science began a journey that continues to amaze, disturb, and enlighten today. Under his stewardship the quantum revolution brought to light some of the finest minds of 20th-century physics, a truly astonishing group of brilliant and innovative scientists, who in turn sowed the ideas that have so profoundly changed our world and the way that we attempt to understand it.

The gradual revelation of the quantum nature of the world has resulted in such practical applications as lasers, MRI (magnetic

Here is Bohr, working on an equation with his son, Aage, also a Nobel laureate in physics. (AIP Emilio Segrè Visual Archives, Margrethe Bohr Collection)

resonance imaging) machines, and semiconductors (the basic materials for transistors and chips that today make possible electronic marvels ranging from miniature radios and television sets to digital watches, cell phones, and personal computers). The much talked-about "Information Superhighway" of the not-so-distant future will have at its core an array of technological marvels based on our understanding and application of quantum theory.

Perhaps even more important, quantum theory and quantum mechanics have changed our understanding of nature at a very basic and profound level. That this new understanding is disturbing to many even today is tribute to its fundamentally revolutionary nature.

Will we see yet another revolution in physics, or with the quantum revolution have we come to the end of the story? Today some scientists are still divided in their acceptance of the "Spirit of Copenhagen." Is the quantum theory complete, or will tomorrow bring a new and perhaps more startling revolution?

Whatever the answer to this question, there can be no doubt that in the annals of scientific history, Niels Bohr will continue to stand as a bright beacon. As both scientist and human being he was a man of insatiable curiosity and tremendous perseverance, a man of unusual intellectual talents and love of knowledge. It was a love that he shared with all around him, with a uniquely infectious enthusiasm. Almost alone in the pantheon of great scientific geniuses such as Galileo, Newton, and Einstein, Niels Bohr came most alive, as a thinker and a human being, in the company of others. Few who came in contact with Bohr were not inspired to put forth their best and develop their deepest thoughts. Out of this exciting interaction, the give and take, inventiveness and criticism, came some of the most profound ideas of our time. And out of it too came a gallery of great thinkers and scientists. Whether students, friends, or coworkers (and often many were all three at the same time), all who knew and worked with Bohr carried with them forever afterward a part of the Bohr legacy.

CHRONOLOGY

October 7, 1885	Niels Bohr is born in Copenhagen, Denmark.
1895	J. J. Thomson discovers the electron.
1896	Nobel Prize established
1900	Quantum theory is established with Planck discovery.
December 5, 1901	Werner Heisenberg is born in Wurzburg, Germany.
1905	Albert Einstein publishes paper on photoelectric effect.
1909	Earns a master's degree in physics from the University of Copenhagen
1910	Ernest Rutherford describes how electrons orbit tiny nuclei in atoms.
1911	Receives a doctorate degree in physics from University of Copenhagen and travels to Cambridge to study at the Cavendish Laboratory headed by Sir Joseph John Thomson
1912	Completes postdoctoral research at the University of Manchester with Ernest Rutherford
May 11, 1912	Marries Margrethe Nørlund

1913	Publishes a trilogy of articles in *Philosophical Magazine* describing his quantum mechanical model of the atom
1914	World War I begins.
1915	Einstein develops his general theory of relativity.
1918	World War I ends.
October 1920	Werner Heisenberg enters the University of Munich.
1921	Becomes the first director of the new Institute for Theoretical Physics in Copenhagen. Retains this position until his death
1922	Fascist government formed in Italy Heisenberg and Bohr meet for the first time at Göttingen lecture series. Receives Nobel Prize in physics on December 11 for his theory of the quantum mechanical model of the atom
1924	Louis de Broglie proposes the wave nature of atoms. Heisenberg begins research at Bohr Institute.
1925	Quantum mechanics first formulated
1926	Erwin Schrødinger proves wave and matrix mechanics mathematically equivalent.
1927	Heisenberg develops uncertainty principle. Bohr and Heisenberg argue for complementary principle at Volta Conference.
1928	Proposes the Copenhagen interpretation

1929 New York City stock market collapses.

1931 Ernest Lawrence and M. Stanley Livingston develop first cyclotron.

1932 James Chadwick discovers neutron.

Heisenberg uses neutron theory to apply quantum mechanics to structure of the nucleus.

1933 Adolf Hitler takes power in Germany in January.

Heisenberg receives Nobel Prize in December.

1934 Enrico Fermi bombards uranium with neutrons in Rome, Italy.

1936–37 Develops liquid droplet model to describe the atomic nucleus

1939 Lise Meitner and Otto Frisch realize that the atom can be split.

Bohr and John Wheeler realize that atomic fission will release great energy.

Bohr helps German-Jewish scientists flee from Germany.

Einstein warns President Roosevelt that Germany may be developing atomic power.

World War II begins in September when Germany invades Poland.

Fermi, now in America, and Frédéric and Irène Joliot-Curie in Paris posit that a nuclear chain reaction is possible.

1940 Otto Frisch and Rudolph Peierls calculate minimum of U-235 needed to sustain chain reaction.

Germany invades Denmark.

1941	Glenn Seaborg and others discover plutonium. In September Heisenberg visits Bohr in Copenhagen.
December 7, 1941	Japan attacks the U.S. base at Pearl Harbor.
1942	Fermi produces first nuclear chain reaction.
1943	Robert Oppenheimer starts work on developing an atomic bomb at Los Alamos.
1943–45	Consults for the Manhattan Project
June 6, 1944	Allied forces arrive in Normandy on D-day.
May 3, 1945	Heisenberg arrested by U.S. forces in Germany.
May 8, 1945	Germany surrenders and the war in Europe ends.
July 16, 1945	The first atomic bomb test succeeds near Alamogordo, New Mexico.
August 6, 1945	An atomic bomb is dropped on Hiroshima, Japan.
August 9, 1945	A second atomic bomb is dropped on Nagasaki, Japan.
August 10, 1945	Japan surrenders.
1962	Niels Bohr dies on November 18th of heart failure at the age of 77 in Copenhagen.

GLOSSARY

alpha particle (alpha rays) one of three types of radiation (the others are beta particles and gamma particles) discovered in early studies of radioactivity around 1900. Rutherford showed that alpha particles are helium nuclei, which are made up of two protons and two neutrons tightly bound together

atom the smallest chemical unit of an element, consisting of a dense, positively charged nucleus surrounded by negatively charged electrons. The Greek thinker Leucippus and his student Democritus originally conceived of the idea of the atom in the 5th century B.C. as the smallest particle into which matter could be divided. (The word "atom" comes from the Greek word *atomos,* which means "indivisible.") But in the 1890s and early 20th century, scientists discovered that the atom is made up of even smaller particles, most of which are very strongly bound together

atomic mass (also known as atomic weight) the relative average mass in atomic mass units (or amu, equal to 1/12 the weight of the isotope carbon-12) of the masses of all the isotopes found in a natural sample of an element

atomic number the number of protons in the nucleus of an atom

atomic spectrum the characteristic pattern produced by light emitted by any element when it is heated

beta particle a high-speed electron (or its positive cousin, the positron) emitted during radioactive decay

complementarity the existence of different aspects of the description of a physical system, seemingly incompatible but both needed for a complete description of the system. In particular, the wave-particle duality (the need to describe some systems as composed of both waves and particles)

cyclotron a device used to accelerate atomic particles around and around in a circle until they reach immense energies

electron a very light, negatively charged subatomic particle that orbits the nucleus of an atom

fission a nuclear reaction in which an atomic nucleus splits into fragments. Fission can generate enormous amounts of energy

isotope one of two or more of any element's atoms with the same number of protons in the nuclei, but a different number of neutrons. Isotopes have the same chemistry but different nuclear physics

neutron an uncharged, or neutral, particle found in the nucleus of every atom except hydrogen. It has nearly the same weight as the proton

photon a small particle, or "packet," of electromagnetic energy, having no mass and no electric charge; electromagnetic force when it behaves as a particle, rather than as a wave. The photon's existence was first proposed by Albert Einstein to explain the behavior of light in photoelectric experiments

Planck's constant (h) the quantity that underlies all of quantum physics. It has the dimensions of momentum times distance or energy times time. It was discovered by Max Planck in 1900 when he tried to explain the spectrum of radiation from a hot body (the "black body radiation problem")

proton a positively charged particle found in the nucleus of all atoms

quanta the plural of "quantum"

quantum [from the Latin adjective meaning "how much"] fundamental unit, or "packet," of energy

quantum theory a theory of atomic and subatomic interaction based on the behavior of all particles as both waves and particles. The theory makes use of the concepts of probability and quantum energy to explain everything that happens on the atomic and subatomic scale

string theory a unified theory of the universe (see TOE) that, unlike the theories of particle physics put forth by Bohr and his colleagues, hypothesizes that the basic ingredients of nature are not particles. Instead, they are extraordinarily tiny one-dimensional filaments called strings. Quantum mechanics and general relativity become compatible in a universe based on string theory, solving the problem of the inconsistencies these two systems precipitate; often short for superstring theory

theory of everything (TOE) a unified theory of the universe that explains otherwise seemingly incompatible phenomena, such as quantum mechanics and general relativity

uranium a heavy, silvery-white radioactive element used in nuclear fuels, nuclear weapons, and research; the heaviest naturally occurring element (atomic number, 238)

X-ray a high-energy photon. X-rays have a very short wavelength and are emitted from a metal target when it is bombarded by energetic electrons

FURTHER RESOURCES

Works by Niels Bohr

Bohr, Niels. *Atomic Physics and Human Knowledge.* New York: John Wiley, 1958.

This collection of articles forms a sequel to earlier essays edited by the Cambridge University Press, 1934, in a volume titled Atomic Theory and the Description of Nature.

———. *Atomic Theory and the Description of Nature.* Cambridge, England: Cambridge University Press, 1961.

Contains an introductory survey of atomic theory and mechanics, the quantum postulate and the recent development of atomic theory, the quantum of action and the description of nature, and the atomic theory and the fundamental principles underlying the description of nature.

———. *Collected Works,* vols. 1–10. Amsterdam: North-Holland, from 1972.

A 10-volume set of Niels Bohr's collected works.

———. "Determination of the Surface-Tension of Water by the Method of Jet Vibration." *Philosophical Transactions of the Royal Society,* 209 (1909), pp. 281ff.

Niels Bohr's first published paper, which came out in 1909.

———. "Disintegration of Heavy Nuclei." *Nature,* 143 (1939), pp. 330ff.

Bohr explores the newly discovered process of fission, beginning with the disintegration of heavy nuclei.

———. *Essays 1958–1963 on Atomic Physics and Human Knowledge.* New York: Interscience, 1963.

Bohr continues his series of essays on atomic physics, from 1958–1963.

———. "Neutron Capture and Nuclear Constitution." *Nature* 137 (1939), pp. 344ff.

As Bohr develops his theory of the atom, he considers the capture of neutrons and the constitution of neutrons.

———. "Resonance in Uranium and Thorium Disintegrations and the Phenomenon of Nuclear Fission." *Physical Review,* 56 (1939), pp. 418ff.

Niels Bohr's take on atomic fission.

———, and J. A. Wheeler. "The Mechanism of Nuclear Fission." *Physical Review,* 56 (1939), pp. 426ff.

Bohr and Wheeler explore the mechanism of nuclear fission in the year it was discovered.

Books about Niels Bohr

French, A. P., and P. J. Kennedy, (editors). *Niels Bohr: A Centenary Volume.* Cambridge, MA: Harvard University Press, 1985.

As well done and fascinating as the Einstein Centenary volume, with many personal reminiscences of Bohr the scientist and Bohr the man.

Moore, Ruth. *Niels Bohr: The Man, His Science, and the World They Changed.* New York: Alfred A. Knopf, 1966.

Straightforward and readable biography of Bohr.

Ottaviani, Jim, Leland Purvis, et al. *Suspended in Language: Niels Bohr's Life, Discoveries, and the Century He Shaped.* Ann Arbor, Mich.: G. T. Labs, 2004.

A clever and witty approach not only for learning about the fascinating life of Niels Bohr but also for gaining a uniquely presented insight into quantum mechanics and the other scientists who changed the way we look at the world. It is all wonderfully told in the style of the best graphic novels but delivers the additional punch of being imaginative and intellectually exciting.

Pais, Abraham. *Niels Bohr's Times: In Physics, Philosophy, and Polity.* New York: Oxford University Press, 1991.

Somewhat complicated in structure and approach but overall the best and most detailed of the books on Bohr to date.

Rozental, S. (editor). *Niels Bohr: His Life and Work as Seen by His Friends and Colleagues.* New York: John Wiley, 1967.

Highly personal reminiscences by those who knew him. Easy to read and often charming.

Segrè, Gino. *Faust in Copenhagen: A Struggle for the Soul of Physics.* New York: Viking, 2007.

A compelling look at the brilliantly individual men and women who through arguments, challenges, grueling all-night discussions, and years of eccentric teamwork put together the pieces of quantum mechanics.

Books about Physics and Physicists of Bohr's Time

Boorse, Henry A., Lloyd Motz, and Jefferson Hane Weaver. *The Atomic Scientists: A Biographical History.* New York: John Wiley, 1989.

Despite its slightly difficult structure and some occasional tough going there is much to be gleaned from this excellent book. Recommended for higher-level readers.

Cline, Barbara Lovett. *Men Who Made a New Physics.* Chicago: University of Chicago Press, 1987.

Well structured and easy-to-read look at the scientists involved in the exciting early days of the quantum revolution. (Published in 1965 by Thomas C. Crowell and Co., New York, as The Questioners.*)*

Cassidy, David C. *Uncertainty: The Life and Times of Werner Heisenberg.* New York: W. H. Freeman and Co., 1992.

A major biography of the still-controversial Heisenberg, probably best for higher-level readers.

Crease, Robert P., and Charles C. Mann. *The Second Creation: Makers of Revolution in 20th-Century Physics.* New York: Macmillan, 1986.

Covers much of the same material as the Cline book, but in more detail and at a deeper level. Best for older readers.

French, A. P. *Einstein: A Centenary Volume.* Cambridge, MA: Harvard University Press, 1979.

Wonderful selection of articles on Einstein the man and the scientist.

Frisch, Otto. *What Little I Remember.* Cambridge: Cambridge University Press. 1979. Reprinted Canto, 1991.

A modest title for an intriguing and readable little book by one of the participants in the history of the early quantum revolution.

Gamow, George. *The Great Physicists From Galileo to Einstein.* New York: Dover Publications, 1988.

The great Gamow takes a look at some major historical physicists and their work. As always with Gamow, readable and enlightening.

———. *Thirty Years That Shook Physics.* New York: Doubleday, 1966.

A highly readable classic, but now a little dated.

Gilmore, Robert. *Alice in Quantumland: An Allegory of Quantum Physics.* New York: Copernicus, 1995.

This clever volume provides an entertaining and accessible introduction to quantum physics.

Goldsmith, Donald, with Robert Libbon. *The Ultimate Einstein.* Includes CD-ROM on the life and work of Einstein. New York: Byron Press Multimedia Books, 1997.

All in all, this is an excellent package introducing Einstein and his ideas—well thought out and easy to digest.

Han, M. Y. *The Probable Universe.* Blue Ridge Summit, PA: Tab Books, 1993.

Han follows up his successful book The Secret Life of the Quanta *with a closer look at the mysteries and controversies as well as the theoretical and technological successes of quantum physics.*

———. *The Secret Life of the Quanta.* Blue Ridge Summit, PA: Tab Books, 1990.

Coming at the quanta from a practical rather than theoretical approach, Han concentrates on explaining how our knowledge of the quanta allows us to build such high-tech devices as computers, lasers, and the CAT scan. At the same time, he doesn't neglect either the theoretical or bizarre aspects of his subject.

Heisenberg, Werner. *Encounters with Einstein.* Princeton, NJ: Princeton University Press, 1989.

Intriguing firsthand look at one great scientist by another.

Hoffmann, Banish. *Albert Einstein: Creator and Rebel.* New York: Viking Press, 1972.

One of the best, most reliable, and most readable studies of the thought and style of the great scientist.

———. *The Strange Story of the Quantum.* New York: Dover Publications, 1959.

A highly readable classic, if a little dated today.

Isaacson, Walter. *Einstein: His Life and Universe.* New York: Simon & Schuster, 2007.

This recent biography offers a good look at both Einstein the person and his work.

Jones, Roger S. *Physics for the Rest of Us.* Chicago: Contemporary Books, 1992.

Informative, nonmathematical discussions of relativity and quantum theory told in a straightforward manner, along with discussions on how both affect our lives and philosophies. Very readable and recommended.

Jungk, Robert. *Brighter Than a Thousand Suns: A Personal History of the Atomic Scientists.* New York: Harcourt, Brace and Co., 1956.

A not always reliable anecdotal account.

Lederman, Leon, with Dick Teresi. *The God Particle.* Boston: Houghton Mifflin Co., 1993.

Highly readable and entertaining discussion of contemporary physics by the witty Nobel Prize-winning physicist.

Lindley, David. *Uncertainty: Einstein, Heisenberg, Bohr, and the Struggle for the Soul of Science.* New York: Doubleday, 2007.

This overview of the uncertainty principle provides an excellent look at the characters and personalities of three of the most intriguing scientists of their time and the meaning of the argument between them.

McCormmach, Russell. *Night Thoughts of a Classical Physicist.* Cambridge, MA: Harvard University Press, 1982.

A fascinating novel treating the mind and emotions of a physicist in Germany who attempts to understand the disturbing changes in physics and the world. It may be loosely based on

Paul Ehrenfest, a friend of both Einstein and Bohr, who committed suicide in 1933.

Moore, Walter. *Schrödinger: Life and Thought.* Cambridge: Cambridge University Press, 1992.

A major biography of the always intriguing and often controversial scientist, for higher-level readers.

Morris, Richard. *Dismantling the Universe.* New York: Simon and Schuster, 1983.

A nontechnical and highly readable look at the thoughts and development that went into creating modern physics. As with other books by Morris, clear-headed and worthwhile.

———. *The Nature of Reality.* New York: McGraw-Hill Book Co., 1987.

A clearly written and tough-minded look at some of the stranger implications of modern physics.

Pagels, Heinz R. *The Cosmic Code: Quantum Physics as the Language of Nature.* New York: Simon and Schuster, 1982.

One of the best books on the subject, clearly and intriguingly written by the late Heinz Pagels, one of the most gifted of the modern writer-scientists.

Pais, Abraham. *Inward Bound: Of Matter and Forces in the Physical World.* Oxford: Clarendon Press, 1986.

Thoughtful and insightful but a little on the difficult side.

———. *Subtle Is the Lord: The Science and Life of Albert Einstein.* New York: Oxford University Press, 1982.

Occasionally tough going, but an excellent look at Einstein's thought and work.

Peat, David F. *Einstein's Moon: Bell's Theorem and the Curious Quest for Quantum Reality.* Chicago: Contemporary Books, 1990.

Intriguing but occasionally difficult look at some of the stranger implications of the quantum world. Well worth sticking with through some of its tougher passages.

Ponomarev, L. I. *The Quantum Dice.* Philadelphia: Institute of Physics Publishing, 1993.

A totally engrossing and well-conceived look at the history of atomic and quantum science.

Pullman, Bernard. Translated by Axel Reisinger. *The Atom in the History of Human Thought.* New York: Oxford University Press, 1998.

Pullman provides a fine overall picture of historical thinking about the atom as well as current concepts.

Rosenblum, Bruce, and Fred Kuttner. *Quantum Enigma: Physics Encounters Consciousness.* Oxford: Oxford University Press, 2006.

Rosenblum and Kuttner offer an interesting but somewhat difficult account of quantum mysteries.

Rothman, Tony. *Everything's Relative and Other Fables from Science and Technology.* Hoboken, N.J.: John Wiley & Sons, Inc., 2003.

Rothman's crisp, snappy, and informative presentation makes this volume fun to read as well as informative.

———. *A Physicist on Madison Avenue.* Princeton: Princeton University Press, 2007.

This is physics for all, presented in an entertaining way. Rothman is superb at getting the more complicated concepts across.

Smolen, Lee. *The Trouble with Physics: The Rise of String Theory, the Fall of a Science, and What Comes Next.* New York: Houghton Mifflin Company, 2006.

This sound, up-to-date book provides a look at string theory, the most traveled hunting grounds for physicists for the last 30 years. Smolen looks at the history and present state of string theory and asks, "Is it on the right road?"

Internet Resources

Bohr, Niels. Banquet Speech. Available online. URL: http://nobelprize.org/nobel_prizes/physics/laureates/1922/bohr-speech.html. Accessed May 14, 2007.

The speech was given by Niels Bohr at the Nobel banquet in Stockholm on December 10, 1922.

———. "The Constitution of Atoms and Molecules." Published originally in *Philosophical Magazine* 1913. Available online. URL: http://dbhs.wvusd.k12.ca.us/webdocs/Chem-History/Bohr/Bohr-1913a.html. Accessed May 14, 2007.

This challenging paper requires a strong knowledge of math but is also worth a look for Bohr's style of writing and thinking.

———. "The Structure of the Atom." Available online. URL: http://nobelprize.org/nobel_prizes/physics/laureates/1922/bohr-lecture.html. Accessed May 14, 2007.

Bohr's Nobel Prize speech.

NBI (Niels Bohr Institute) History. Available online. URL: http://www.nbi.dk/nbi-history.html. Accessed May 14, 2007.

The Niels Bohr Institute history page has extensive information on the institute itself, but the site is of primary interest for the many brief but informative entries on Bohr's life and works. It also includes concise but valuable information on the early days of atomic physics and quantum theory.

The Niels Bohr Archives. Available online. URL: http://www.nba.nbi.dk/. Accessed May 14, 2007.

This site lists the papers, photographs, letters, and other documents held by the archives. The site provides a brief description of the Bohr-Heisenberg controversy and a description of the letters related to it that have been released by the archives. Most of the material cannot be viewed on the Web site but must be requested by contacting the archives, but some of Bohr's correspondence on the subject is open to the viewer.

"Niels Bohr: The Nobel Prize in Physics, 1922." Nobelprize.org. Biography from *Nobel Lectures. Physics 1922–1941.* Elsevier Publishing Company, Amsterdam, 1965. Available online. URL: http://nobelprize.org/nobel prizes/physics/lauretes/1922/bohr-bio.html. Accessed May 14, 2007.

"Niels Bohr. Physicist." Available online. URL: http://www.lucidecafe.com/library/95oct/nbohr.html. Accessed May 14, 2007.

In addition to a brief biographical profile, this site offers links to multiple Web pages featuring Niels Bohr and his work.

"Niels Bohr." A Science Odyssey: People and Discoveries. PBS: Public Broadcasting Service. Available online. URL: http://www.pbs.org/wgbh/aso/databank/entries/bpbohr.html. Accessed May 14, 2007.

This site provides a biographical sketch issued as part of the Internet site coverage of the People and Discoveries program series.

"Niels Bohr." Wikipedia, the free encyclopedia. Available online. URL: http://en.wikipedia.org/wiki/Niels_Bohr. Accessed May 14, 2007.

The Wikipedia encyclopedia entry on Bohr contains much interesting information relating to just about anything you may want to know about Bohr but, as with all Wikipedia pages, it is important to double-check the information with other sources before using it. Wikipedia also has an interesting list of links, although some may be outdated and no longer available.

"Niels Henrik David Bohr" Mactutor History of Mathematics Archives. Turnbull WWW Server, School of Mathematical and Computational Sciences, University of St Andrew. Available online. URL: http://www-groups.dcs.st-nd.ac.uk/~history/Mathematicians/Bohr_Niels.html. Accessed May 14, 2007.

This interesting site has a large list of references (articles and books) relating to Bohr as well as quotations from Bohr and links to other material.

Nobelprize.org. Available online. URL: http://nobelprize.org/nobel_prizes/physics/lauretes/1922/bohr-bio.html. Accessed May 14, 2007.

This Web site sponsored by the Nobel Prize Committee offers, in addition to a brief biography of Niels Bohr, his Nobel Prize lecture, banquet speech, and links to other resources.

PBS (Public Broadcasting Service) Hollywood Presents: *Copenhagen.* Available online. URL: http://www.pbs.org/hollywoodpresents/copenhagen/story/bohr.html. Accessed May 14, 2007.

This PBS Web site supplements the production Copenhagen, *the intriguing play relating to the Bohr-Heisenberg meeting in 1941 and the controversy and mystery that ensued. It describes the moral dilemma presented by the meeting and brief biographies of the people represented in the play, including Bohr's wife Margrethe.*

"Scientist: Niels Bohr." Answers.com. Available online. URL: http://www.answers.com/topic/niels-bohr. Accessed May 15, 2007.

This helpful page of information on Bohr from Answers.com gives biographies from many different sites directly on their page without needing to use outside links.

INDEX

Italic page numbers indicate illustrations

A

absorption spectra 46, 47, *47*
alpha particles 25, 27, 31, 34, 72, 73
alpha rays 25
aluminum 31
Andersen, Hans Christian 19
Andrade, E. 31, 32
anomalous Zeeman effect 61
argon gas 27
arms race 96, 101
atom
  ancient Greek concept of 13–15
  Bohr model 49–52, *50*
  Bohr's research on structure xiv, 35–36
  and discovery of radiation 15
  proton-neutron model of nucleus 73–74
  quantum theory and atomic structure 43, 49–51
  Rutherford model 27–29, *28*, 35–36, 43, 49
  splitting of uranium 85, 88
  Thomson model 15, 28, *28*
  and wave-particle duality 62
atomic bomb xvi, 86–91, 93–99
atomic collisions 63
Atomic Energy Commission (Denmark) 102
atomic mass 73
atomic nucleus *26*, 28–29, 73–74
atomic number 32
atomic particles 72–74, 76. *See also specific particles, e.g.:* neutrons
atomic structure 48–49, 72–74, 76. *See also* atomic nucleus
atomic theory, early 13–14
atomic weight 32
Atoms for Peace Award 102–103

B

Balmer, Johann 46, 47
barium 88
Becquerel, Henri 14, 15
Bell, John S. 78
Berlin Physical Society 40
beryllium 73
beta particle 25, 34
beta rays 25
black body radiation 39–41
Bohr, Aage 88, 90, 93, 96, 98, *114*
Bohr, Christian 81
Bohr, Ellen Adler 6–8, *7*, 79–80
Bohr, Harald *7*, *11*
  childhood experiences 5–8
  correspondence from Niels Bohr 24, 34, 35
  death of 103
  and death of Jenny Bohr 80
  letter to UN 98
  on Niels Bohr's teaching style 9
  and Niels Bohr's wedding 38
  and outbreak of World War I xv

postgraduate work 15–18
and reaction to Bohr's atomic theory 51
at University of Copenhagen 10
Bohr, Henrik George Christian 6–9, 12, 18
Bohr, Jenny 7, *7*, 9–10, 80
Bohr, Margrethe (Nørlund) *16*, 17–19, 37–38, 89, 95
Bohr, Niels *7, 11, 16, 55, 65, 72, 74, 87, 92, 97*
atomic model 49–52, *50*
atomic structure research 35–36
atomic structure trilogy 48–49
Atoms for Peace Award 102–103
childhood and early education 6–10
children of 53
complementarity principle 65
compound nucleus theory 76
death of 105–106
debate over quantum theory 77–78
depicted in *Copenhagen* 89
doctoral thesis work 18–19
early research 12
and Einstein 3–5, 55–56, 66–68
escape from occupied Denmark 88, 90
Faust parody 75–76
Frisch's description of 58
and Heisenberg's involvement with German nuclear program xvi, 86–87, 89
Institute for Advanced Study 1–5
Institute for Theoretical Physics 53–59
legacy of 113–115
in Manchester 52–53
and Manhattan Project 90–91, 93
master's thesis work 15
postgraduate work with Rutherford in Manchester 24, 29–36
postgraduate work with Thomson in Cambridge 20–24
radioactivity research 32, 34
teaching post at University of Copenhagen 53–54
theoretical physics 30
wave-particle duality 64
wedding of 37–38
world peace promotion 94–99
Bolund Island 101–102
Born, Max xv, 63, 64, 108
boson 110
British Royal Society 12
Broglie, Louis de 62–63
Brownian motion 42

C

calculus 110
Cambridge University 13
Carlsberg Beer Company 55
Carlsberg House 76–77, 95
Cassidy, David C. 87, 89
cathode rays 13, 22
causality 63
cause and effect, quantum mechanics and 108
Cavendish Laboratory 13, 20–25, 27, 55
CERN (European Council for Nuclear Research) 100, 104
Chadwick, James 73
Chievitz, Ole 9, 81
Chita (yacht) 81

Christiansen, Christian 38
Churchill, Winston 91, 93, 95
classical mechanics 39, 63, 77–78
clock-in-a-box thought experiment 66–68, *67*
cloud chamber 29–30
Cockcroft, John 74
color, photoelectric effect and 42
complementarity 65, 78–79, 103, 106
compound nucleus 76
Copenhagen (drama) xvi, 89
Courant, Richard 17, 68–69
Curie, Marie 14–15, 25, 107

D

Danish Academy of Technical Sciences 101
Danish Royal Academy of Sciences and Literature 105
Darwin, Charles Galton 34
Democritus 14, 15
determinism 63
Dickens, Charles 22
Dirac, Paul 59, 80
Drude, Paul 17
duality 10, 62–63

E

Ehrenfest, Paul 51, 56, 80
Einstein, Albert *65*, *79*
  on Bohr's atomic model 50–51
  and Bohr's lectures at *Physikalische Gesellschaft* 55–56
  on Bohr's search for scientific truth 106
  death of 103
  and Ehrenfest's suicide 80
  general theory of relativity 42, 110
  and Institute for Advanced Study 2, 103
  leaves Germany xvi
  meets Bohr 55–56
  on Pauli's relativity article 60
  on quantum mechanics 63–64
  and quantum theory 41, 66
  relationship with Bohr xv, 3–5, 77–78, 106
  special theory of relativity 41–42, 110
  theory of everything 108
  and Uncertainty Principle 64
  wave-particle duality 62
Eisenhower, Dwight D. 101–103
electron 13–15
  and alpha particles 34
  and characteristics of metals 15
  orbit of 43, 46–47, 56, 62
  and Pauli's Exclusion Principle 62
  and problems with Rutherford's atomic model 35–36
  and Thomson's atomic model 28
  and Uncertainty Principle 64
  and wave-particle duality 62, 63
electron theory of metals 15, 18–19
$E=mc^2$ 41–42
emission spectra 43–47, *44*
Encyclopedia of Mathematical Sciences, The 60
energy
  discontinuous nature of 40
  and electron orbits 46–47
  and special theory of relativity 42
EPR thought experiment 77–78
Exclusion Principle. *See* Pauli's Exclusion Principle
experimental physics 30–31

F

Faust, physicists' parody of 75–76
fermion 110
Feynman, Richard 68
fission 89
fluorescence 14
Franck, James *74*
Frankfurter, Felix 91, 93
Frayn, Michael 89
Frisch, Otto
  on Bohr as teacher 58
  on Bohr at 50 77
  on Bohr's problem-solving skills 31
  on Bohr's willingness to admit error 106
  on complementarity 65
  and Lise Meitner 83–85
  on quantum physics 49–50
Fuld Hall 1, 2

G

gamma rays 25
Gamow, George 71–72, *72*
Gardner, Martin 109
Geiger, Hans 27, 31, 32
Gell-Mann, Murray 108
general theory of relativity 42, 110
Germany xv–xvi, 104–105. *See also* Nazi Germany
glasnost 99
Goethe, Johann Wolfgang von 6
gold 27
Gorbachev, Mikhail 99
gravity 111
ground state 46

H

Hahn, Otto 83–85, 88
Hansen, Hans Marius *74*
heat, electron orbit and 46
Heisenberg, Werner *72, 87*
  depicted in *Copenhagen* 89
  and German nuclear program 86–87, 89
  at Institute for Theoretical Physics 59
  meeting with Bohr during German occupation of Denmark xvi, 89
  and nucleus model 73–74
  and Uncertainty Principle 64, 66–68, 108
  and wave-particle duality 64
Heisenberg's Uncertainty Principle. *See* Uncertainty Principle
helium, emission spectrum of *44*
heroic age of quantum physics 49, 70
Hevesy, Georg von 31, 50–51, 57
high-energy physics 100–101
Hiroshima 94
Hitler, Adolf xv, 81
Høffding, Harald 10–11
Holocaust xv–xvi, 81
hydrogen *44,* 45, 46
hydrogen bomb 96, 99

I

Indian Science Congress 104
inert gas 27
Institute for Advanced Study 1–4, 61, 79, 103
Institute for Theoretical Physics xiv, 53–59, *57,* 71–74, 102
Institute of Genetics 104
isotope 32, 88

J

Joliot-Curie, Irène and Frédéric 73
Jung, Carl 61

K

Klein, Oskar *72*
Knudsen, Martin 38–39, 53
Korean War 99
Kramers, Hendrik *72*

L

Landau, Lev *72*
Lederman, Leon 63
Leucippus 14, 15

Lie, Trygve 98–99
light 42, 46, 62
"Light and Life Revisited" 104
London *Times* 94–95
Lorentz, Hendrik 13, 17
Los Alamos, New Mexico 90–91, 94
Lynghuset 56–57

M

Manhattan Project 90–93
Marshall, George 96
mass, special theory of relativity and 42
Maxwell, James Clerk 22
McGill University 27
Meitner, Lise 83–85, *84*
Mendeleyev, Dmitry 14
mercury, emission spectrum of *44*
metal, passage of alpha particles through 34
Møller, Poul Martin 10
Mollgaard, Holgar 17
Morrison, Philip 79

N

Nagasaki 94
Nazi Germany 81, 83, 86–89
Nehru, Jawaharal 104
neutron, Rutherford's discovery of 73
Newton, Isaac 110
Newtonian physics 63, 110
New York Herald Tribune, The 99
Nicholson, J. W. 43–45
Niels Bohr Institute. *See* Institute for Theoretical Physics
Nielsen, Jens Rud 38
Nobel Prize
  Bohr xiv, 49
  Einstein 42
  Pauli 62
  Rutherford 27
  Thomson 22
Nordita 100–101
Nørlund, Margrethe. *See* Bohr, Margrethe
nuclear arms race 96, 101
nuclear atom 34
nuclear disarmament xvi
nuclear fission 89
nucleus *26*, 28–29, 73–74, 76, 88

O

Odenwald, Sten 111
"On the Constitution of Atoms and Molecules" (Bohr) 48–49
"On the Quantum Theory of Radiation and the Structure of the Atom" (Bohr) 52
"Open Letter to the United Nations" xvi
Oppenheimer, J. Robert 2, 4, 69–70, 90, *91*
orbits, of electrons 43, 46, 62

P

Pais, Abraham 2–3, 53, 98
paradox 74
particle accelerator 74
particle physics 100–101, 110
Pauli, Wolfgang 3, 59–62, *72*, 75–76, 104
Pauli repulsion 110
Pauli's Exclusion Principle 61–62
Pavillonen 57
peace activism xvi, 94–99, 102–103
periodic table 14, 32, *33*, 34
Philosophical Magazine 38, 48, 52
Philosophical Transactions (British Royal Society journal) 12
photoelectric effect 42–43
photon 46, 62, 66
Physikalische Gesellschaft (Physics Society) 55
Planck, Max 39–41, 43, 55, 62
Planck's constant (h) 40–41, 46, 47
Planck's theorem. *See* quantum theory
Podolsky, Boris 77
potassium, emission spectrum of 45

Princeton, New Jersey. *See* Institute for Advanced Study
probability 63
proton 72–73
proton synchrotron particle accelerator 100

Q

quantum mechanics 39, 43, 63–64, 77–78, 108
quantum/quanta 40–43
quantum theory
  Bohr-Einstein debate 77–78
  Bohr's atomic model 49–51
  Bohr's teaching work at Copenhagen 53
  and complementarity 64–66, 68–70
  and emission spectra *44*
  EPR thought experiment 77–78
  and heroic age of quantum physics 70
  and photoelectric effect 42–43
  Planck's pioneering work 40–41
  practical applications 113–114
  Rutherford's atomic model 43
  and Uncertainty Principle 64

R

radiation, Planck's constant and 40–41
radioactive displacement law 34
radioactive elements 27, 32
radioactive tracers 31
radioactivity 13–15, 27, 32, 34, 72–73
Rayleigh, Lord. *See* Strutt, John William (third baron Rayleigh)
relativistic quantum field theory 110
relativity 41–42, 60, 110
Risø Peninsula 102
Rockefeller Institute 104
Röntgen, Wilhelm Conrad 13, 15
Roosevelt, Franklin Delano 91, 93
Rosen, Nathan 77
Royal Danish Academy of Science and Letters 12
Rutherford, Ernest *25*
  atomic model 27–29, *28*, 49
  and Bohr's atomic model 50
  and Bohr's paper on atomic structure 48–49
  and Bohr's readership at Manchester 52
  and Bohr's University of Copenhagen teaching post 51
  at Carlsberg 76
  at Cavendish 24–27, 55
  death of 80–81
  early work with Bohr 30–36
  in Manchester 27–30, 38, 54
  at McGill University 27
  proton discovery 72–73
Rutherford, Mary 38, 76
Rydberg, Johannes 46, 47

S

Schrödinger, Erwin 59, *62*, 62–63
"Science and Civilization" (newspaper article) 94–95
Six Roads from Newton (Speyer) 78
Snow, C. P. 30
soccer 5
Soddy, Frederick 27, 32, 107
sodium, emission spectrum of *44*, 45
Solvay Conferences 66–68, *72*, 104
Sommerfeld, Arnold xv, 55, 60, 64
Soviet Union 91, 93, 96, 99
spacetime, string theory and 109
special theory of relativity 41–42, 110
spectra. *See* emission spectra
Speyer, Edward 78

stability, of atoms 35–36
stationary states 43
Stern, Otto 66
Strassmann, Fritz 85, 88
string theory xvi, 108–109, 111
Strutt, John William (3rd Baron Rayleigh) 12, 50
superstring theory. *See* string theory
supersymmetry 111
surface tension 12
synchrocyclotron particle accelerator 100
"Systems Containing Only a Single Nucleus" (Bohr) 49
"Systems Containing Only Several Nuclei" (Bohr) 49

T

Tale of a Danish Student (Møller) 10
theoretical physics 30–31
theory of everything (TOE) 108
Thomson, J. J. *21*
  atomic model *28*
  and Bohr's atomic model 50
  and Bohr's master's thesis work 17
  discovery of electron 13–15, 110
  work with Bohr at Cambridge 20–25, 30
thorium 27
thought experiments 66–68, 77–78
Tisvilde 56–57, 95, 105
tracers 31
transformation theory 107–108

U

ultraviolet catastrophe 39–41
ultraviolet radiation 40
Uncertainty Principle 64, 66–68, 78, 108
unified field theory 64
United Nations 97–99, 101
universal constant 40
universe 109–110
University of Berlin 39
University of California 53
University of Copenhagen 6, 8–11, 38–39, 51, 53–54, 60
University of Göttingen 60
University of Manchester 24, 27, 30–36
uranium 9, 14, 82, 85, 88
uranium-235 32, 86

V

Villard, Paul U. 25

W

Walton, Ernest Thomas Sinton 74
Washington Post, The 99
wavelength, photoelectric effect and 42–43
wave mechanics 63
wave-particle duality 62–63
Weisskopf, Victor 90–91
Wilson, C. T. R. 29–30
world peace activism xvi, 94–99, 102–103
World War I xv, 52–53
World War II 81–82, 86–94

X

X-ray 13

Y

Yearbook of Physics 41